GREEK LOVE SONGS
AND EPIGRAMS

Photo. Mansell.

Eros.

GREEK LOVE SONGS
AND EPIGRAMS

FROM THE ANTHOLOGY

TRANSLATED BY

J. A. POTT

Fredonia Books
Amsterdam, The Netherlands

Greek Love Songs and Epigrams:
From the Anthology

Translated by
J. A. Pott

ISBN: 1-58963-814-X

Copyright © 2002 by Fredonia Books

Reprinted from the 1911 edition

Fredonia Books
Amsterdam, The Netherlands
http://www.fredoniabooks.com

PREFACE

THIS little series of versions does not profess
to represent the best epigrams in the Greek
Anthology, being merely an attempt to render
in English verse a few of the poems which
appeal to my personal taste, and seem to lend
themselves to this treatment.

The strict canons of translation laid down
by some authorities—for example, Mr. Arthur
Symonds—are not, I think, applicable to
renderings of Greek Poetry. Not only is it
true that imitations of classical metres are
rarely successful in English, but also that the
elegiac couplet is used for a great variety of
subjects, some of which inevitably suggest the
use of particular measures in our language ;
but if the adoption of French forms such as
the Rondel, Lai, or Triolet be a mistake, at
least I err in excellent company.

The short Notes and Translations therein quoted are gathered from many sources, most of which have, I hope, been acknowledged duly, and I have endeavoured in many instances to call the reader's attention to admirable versions which I have not been able to quote at length. The references at the foot of each epigram are to the Didot Edition of the Palatine Anthology.

In addition to the debt which all readers of the Anthology owe to Jacobs and to the editors of the book above named, I am under special obligations to Professor Murray for permission to print his version from Mimnermus; to Professor Mackail, whom I have often quoted, probably oftener than I know; to the late Dr. Headlam; and to a friend and critic who, with characteristic generosity, refuses to admit my indebtedness.

CONTENTS

CONTENTS

CONTENTS

THE GARLAND OF MELEAGER

The Garland, which is prefixed to this series of translations, formed the preface to a collection of epigrams made by Meleager in the first century B.C. It is much more than a mere enumeration of names, for each poet mentioned has a flower assigned to him which is symbolical of the quality of his work, and thus we have 'many exquisite criticisms conveyed by short phrases,' or even by single words. The comment upon Sappho has passed into a proverb, but there are others at least as happy; and when an emblem seems to fail of appropriateness it must be remembered that we often have to judge a Greek poet's worth from fragments, whilst to Meleager all his work was accessible.

DEAR Muse, for whom dost bring these flowers
    of song?
And whose the hand that wove the poet's
    wreath?
'Twas Meleager wrought it for his friend,
A fair memorial of his love, whereto
Hath Anytè brought lilies divers-hued,

And Moero may blooms, but all her flowers
Are lilies white, and Sappho few but roses.
The sweet narcissus is the choral strain
Of Melanippides, each bud an hymn ;
Here the fresh vine shoot of Simonides
Is twined with Nossis' heavy scented flags,
She for whose tablets love did melt the wax,
With marjoram of Rhiânus fragrant song,
Sweet virgin crocus that Erinna gave,
Alcaeus' hyacinth, the poet's flower
That cries aloud, and Samius' dark-leaved bay.
Leonidas hath clustered ivy leaves,
Mnasalcas needles from the slender pine ;
But from the spreading plane I plucked a spray
For Pamphilus, to twine with walnut shoots
For Pancrates, and fair white poplar leaves
That Tymnes brought, green mint for Nicias
And for Euphêmus poppies of the shore.

But set with these is Damagetus' flower
The purple violet ; and Caliimachus
Hath myrtle berries ever honey-sweet,
Yet with the nectar there is bitterness.
Here is Euphorion's lychnis, and for him
To whom the Dioscuri gave their name
The spice plant of the Muses ; next I wove
The maddening grape for Hegesippus' gift,

And cut a scented rush for Perses' flower :
But Diotîmus hath sweet apple bloom,
Menecrates the young pomegranate bud,
Nicaenetus a sprig of scented myrrh,
And for Phaënnus there is terebinth,
For Simmias the lofty forest pear.
Next, from a mead scarce trodden did I cull
But these few parsley leaves of Parthenis :
And, gleaning where the honeyed Muses passed,
I found thy golden corn, Bacchylides.

This is Anacreon's flower, wild eglantine,
From that sweet song and nectarous elegies ;
And yonder whitethorn from a tangled brake,
Like salt sea foam, is for Archilochus.
Herewith are Alexander's olive shoots,
And Polycleitus' cornflower purple hued
But for Polystratus, the flower of bards,
I set sweet rosemary ; and here I wove
Young Tyrian cypress for Antipater,
With sharp-leaved nard that loves the Syrian
     land
For one that sang himself as Hermes' gift,
Wild blossoms from the corn for Hedylus
And Posidippus, but Sicelides
Hath the frail flowers begotten of the wind.
Yea, and with these is set the golden bough

Of Plato ever godlike, and it shines
Bright in its virtue over all the world.
But for Aratus since he knew the stars,
I cut fresh sprays grown from an heaven high
        palm.

Chaerêmon hath the fair-tressed lotus cup,
Wherewith are gilly-flowers for Phaedimus,
And curvèd oxeyes for Antagoras.
Here is the gift of Theodorides,
Wild thyme, fresh blown, the herb that loves
        the wine,
And Phanias hath the blossom of the bean.
With these be many sprays of other flowers
Entwined for later singers—but for me
Early white violets my Muse hath culled.
Mine own fair gift is woven for my friends,
But all who know the mysteries may share
The Muses' wreath, this garland of sweet song.

ALCMAN

*Alcman, whose name is the Doric form of
Alcmaeon, was a Laconian, and flourished about
650 B.C. ; according to Athenian writers he came
from Lydia, for they refused to assign a Spartan
origin to any poet.   One of his fragments is
well known through the imitations of it in ' In
Memoriam,' and in ' Love in Idleness.'   The
last-named version is given below :—*

Maidens with voices like honey for sweetness
    that breathe desire,
Would that I were a sea-bird with wings that
    never could tire,
Over the foam flowers flying, with halcyons
    ever on wing,
Keeping a careless heart, a sea-blue bird of
    the spring.

*The fragment here translated is part of a
description of a still night in the vale of Lace-
daemon, and the original breaks off abruptly at
line 7.*

NIGHT IN THE VALLEY

SLEEP broods o'er the mountain crest,
    And the folds of the hill,
Hollow and headland rest,
    Silent and still.

All things are slumbering,
    Not a leaf is stirred,
From insect or creeping thing
    No rustle is heard.
The beasts of the mountain sleep,
    And the murmuring bees,
And the monsters that haunt the deep
    Of the purple seas ;
The swift winged tribes of the air
    Have ceased from their flight . .

BERGK. Fr. 61

MIMNERMUS

Mimnermus of Colophon has two epigrams in the Anthology, one of which, an epitaph upon Hipponax, is also attributed to Philip. His date is about 630 B.C., so he would be a younger contemporary of Alcman and Archilochus, and may have lived till the time of Sappho, Alcaeus, and Solon : only fragments of his work remain, and the passage here translated is not taken from the Palatine Anthology but will be found in Bergk's 'Anthologia Lyrica.' The simile in the first line, which is also used by Simonides (see p. 14), is taken from Homer.

The most striking of the extant fragments has been finely translated by Professor Murray :—

Surely the Sun has labour all his days
    And never any respite, steeds, nor god,
Since Eos first, whose hands are rosy rays,
    Ocean forsook, and Heaven's high pathway
      trod :
At night across the sea that wondrous bed
    Shell hollow, beaten by Hephaestus' hand,
Of winged gold and gorgeous, bears his head
    Half waking on the wave, from eve's red strand
To the Ethiop shore, where steeds and chariot are,
    Keen mettled, waiting for the morning star.

AS THE FLOWERS OF THE GRASS

WE are as leaves in jewelled springtime
    growing
  That open to the sunlight's quickening rays ;
So joy we in our span of youth, unknowing
  If God shall bring us good or evil days.

Two fates beside thee stand ; the one hath
    sorrow,
  Dull age's fruit, that other gives the boon
Of Death, for youth's fair flower hath no to-
    morrow,
  And lives but as a sunlit afternoon.

And when thine hour is spent, and passeth by
    thee,
  Surely to die were better than to live,
Ere grief or evil fortune come anigh thee,
  And penury that hath but ill to give.

Who longs for children's love, for all his yearn-
    ing
  Shall haply pass to death anhungered still ;
Or pain shall come, his life to anguish turning,
  Zeus hath for all an endless store of ill.

BERGK, Anth. Lyr. v. 2.

ANACREON

Anacreon was a native of Teos in Ionia, but after the Persian invasion of 540 B.C. settled in Thrace and afterwards lived under the patronage of various princes in Samos, Athens, and Thessaly. His death in 478 B.C., when he was eighty-five years old, was caused, according to tradition, by a grape-stone which choked him—an invention probably suggested by the poet's evident devotion to the wine god.

The genuine fragments of his work are few, and of the epigrams in the Anthology none are certainly authentic, though little is to be said against the epitaph upon Timocritus. The poem on Eros bound with roses is quoted by Leopardi, who professes to have found it in a MS. at Rome. The late imitations of his work have been popularised through the versions of Herrick, Cowley, John Addison, Moore and others, but these probably convey a one-sided impression of the character of his poetry as a whole. Herrick's delightful lyric upon Cupid stung by a bee is too well known to be quoted at length, and there is another and less familiar version of the same Anacreontic in Mr. Bullen's 'Elizabethan Lyrics.'

'*UNSOWN HONEYSUCKLE*'

TOO OLD

'TIS Eros of the golden hair
Doth challenge us his game to share,
And throws his purple ball,
Displaying every trick and wile,
For thus our hearts would he beguile
To answer to his call.
But, ah, 'tis all in vain, for she,
My Lesbian maid, despises me ;
My locks her anger stir :
A hoary head doth she disdain,
And so she seeks a younger swain
To play the game with her.

Ap. Athen. XIII. 599.

LOVE'S MOCKERY

BENEATH a leafy shade
A little Love was laid,
    Sleeping I found him,
And softly stealing there
I bound a fetter fair
    Of roses round him.
But soon the child awoke,
The flowery bond he broke
    And said, 'My master,
Thou shouldst not so be free
If I had fettered thee,
    My bonds hold faster!

EPITAPH ON TIMOCRITUS

SINCE he was bold, his guerdon was the grave
Ares who spares the coward, slays the brave.

                                        II. 160.

SIMONIDES

Simonides of Ceos, whose emblem is the vine shoot, was born in Iulis in 556 B.C., and during a long life, for he lived to be nearly ninety years old, he maintained a reputation as wit, poet, and sage which placed him in popular esteem above even Pindar. The latter poet was according to tradition jealous of Simonides' reputation and success, but the accusations of ingratitude and venality made against him have but little foundation. Anyhow, 'when all Hellas stood upon the razor's edge,' Simonides threw his influence upon the side of freedom, whilst Pindar was unfaithful to the cause of Greece.

His most celebrated inscription is the couplet upon the Spartans who fell at Thermopylae, which, as has been said, almost made Cicero, who translated it, a poet.

Bowles' version of this, which Christopher North calls perfect, runs thus :—

> Go tell the Spartans, thou that passest by,
> That here obedient to their laws we lie.

Amongst the ninety poems still extant there are other epitaphs at least equal to this, and the fragment upon those who died with Leonidas ' whose grave is an altar, and their dirge a song

*of praise,' is magnificent in its nobility and
restraint, whilst the poem upon Danäe afloat
with her child at night is the very perfection of
pathos. Perhaps this fragment was in Words-
worth's mind when he wrote of ' Some precious
tender-hearted scroll of pure Simonides,' and
reading it one wonders that Lessing should have
compared the author with Voltaire, unless the
criticism refers to Simonides' world-wide reputation and authority.*

*It is supposed that the first two epigrams here
translated were intended for the graves of those
who fell at Plataea. The MS., however, gives the
title ' On those who fell with Leonidas,' and this
heading is adopted by some commentators.*

'VINE SHOOTS'

THE DEAD AT PLATAEA

I

IN sooth if valour's noblest part be this,
    Nobly to die,
By fate's award the prize we shall not miss,
    For here we lie ;
Striving to crown our land with Freedom's bays,
    Death we disdained,
And Time shall never mar the meed of praise
    That valour gained.

II

The land they loved shall wear the fadeless
    crown
            Her warriors gave her,
When, wrapped in death's dark cloud, they laid
    them down
            Dying to save her.
Yet being dead they die not, in the grave
            Tho' they be lying,
These be the souls to whom high valour gave
            Glory undying.

                                    VII. 251.

'SE A TE VUOI ESSER BUONO'

NAUGHT amongst men unshaken may abide,
    And soothly doth the sage of Chios sing
    'The race of man is as the leaves of Spring';
Yet though we hear, we thrust the truth aside,
Nor ponder it, for Hope is still our guide,
    Fond Hope to which young hearts will ever
        cling :
    Youth recks not, in his flower, of languishing,
But sows vain dreams to die unsatisfied :

For age seems far and dim, and farther Death
  And whole, men deem not life may fade and
          wane,
  Ah fools and blind that have not under-
          stood
How youth is brief, how life is but a breath ;
  Thou that are better taught, while life re-
          main
  Strive still for this, to sate thy soul with
          good.

                              App. IV. 3.

PLATO

Plato (427-347 B.C.) appears in the Anthology as the author of thirty-two epigrams, most of which are of doubtful authenticity. Four of these have been translated by Shelley, whose version of Ep. V. 78 is, however, rather an expanded paraphrase than a translation. His version of the lines to Aster is given below as being ‘ the best version of the best epigram ever written.’ The poem upon the sleeping faun is perhaps by Antipater of Sidon, and that upon Laïs' Mirror is by some attributed to Julian of Egypt. The lines upon the Eretrian exiles, who were removed from Euboea by Datis during the first Persian war, may be genuine, and are quoted by Philostratus in his life of Apollonius of Tyana.

Epigram VI. 1 (p. 17) was translated by Ausonius, from whose version Prior took his well-known lines. A pretty imitation of the same little poem is quoted by Mr. Bullen (‘ Lyrics from the Elizabethan Song-books ’), and is given below :—

To Aster

Thou wert the Morning Star amongst the living
    Ere thy pure light had fled :
Now, having died, thou art as Hesperus giving
    New lustre to the dead.

SHELLEY.

Laïs' Mirror

Lais, now old, that once all-tempting lass
To Goddess Venus dedicates her glass,
For she herself hath now no use of one,
No dimpled cheek hath she to gaze upon.
She cannot see her springtide damask grace,
Nor dare she look upon her winter face.

' *THE GOLDEN BOUGH* '

ON A SILVER STATUE OF A SLEEPING FAUN

'Twas Diodorus charmed the faun to sleep,
        He did not make him.
The silver holds him wrapped in slumber deep
        A touch may wake him.

                            XVI. 248.

AN OFFERING TO APHRODITE

I laughed exultant over men,
    All Hellas sighed for longing ;
Young gallants sought for Laïs then,
    About her portal thronging.

But now I bring my glass to Thee,
    To look therein I care not ;
For what I was I cannot see,
    And what I am I dare not.

                            VI. I.

B

'AN INVITATION'

LIE here 'neath the murmuring trees,
Where the pine on high doth whisper and sigh
At the kiss of the western breeze;
And the song of the babbling streams,
With the pipe's soft note, through your soul
    shall float
And lull you to magic dreams.

XVI. 13.

DEATH IN EXILE

FAR from the thunder and surge of our own
    Aegean wave,
  Here in Ecbatana's plain found we a grave.
Farewell to our glorious city; Athens, farewell
    to thee,
  Who art near to our native isle—farewell,
    dear sea.

VII. 256.

ADDAEUS

Addaeus of Macedon, who belongs to the second half of the fourth century B.C., is represented by eleven epigrams, five of which are sepulchral and include epitaphs upon Philip, Alexander the Great, and Euripides. Other of his verses deal with country life, and from these has been drawn the conclusion that the author was a country gentleman. The former epigram here translated refers to a kindly custom of sparing plough oxen : in some states it was illegal, in early days, to sacrifice them.

'OUR BROTHER THE OX'

WORN was the ox with years and the weight of
    a toilsome life,
But Alcon revered his work and spared him the
    butcher's knife.
Henceforth in the pasture deep he shall wander
    at will, and now
He lows in gladness of heart to be free from the
    heavy plough.

VI. 228.

PERSES

Perses, who probably flourished during the fourth century B.C., was the author of nine epigrams in the Anthology, and his emblem is the scented rush. Tycho, the god of good luck, is identified with Priapus.

THE GOD OF LITTLE THINGS

HIM will I aid that doth my power invoke,
    But ask not much, 'tis little things I sway ;
For I am Tycho of the common folk,
    And give to labouring men what boons I may.

IX. 334.

SIMMIAS

Simmias of Rhodes is the nominal author of twelve poems in the Anthology, but three of these are wrongly attributed to him. In two other cases the title represents the author as Simmias the Theban, but this is probably a mistake made by some editor or copyist who confused the poet with Socrates' disciple.

The Rhodian writer flourished about 300 B.C. and is represented in the Garland by the lofty forest pear. Besides epigrams he wrote certain curious poems whose text was set in fanciful shapes, one being called from its form ' the wings of Eros,' and another ' the axe.'

English readers will remember how Herrick also dealt in these toys, which are called Figurata.

The epitaph on Sophocles is well known through an anonymous version which appeared in the ' Spectator.'

'WILD PEAR'

'WHO SAW LIFE STEADILY, AND SAW IT WHOLE'

SOFTLY, O ivy, softly creep,
He is asleep ;
Thy fair pale tendrils gently spread
Above his head.

O roses, let your blossoms grace
            His resting-place.
Ye tender vine leaves weave a shade
            Where he is laid.
The Graces wrought the songs he sung
            With honeyed tongue,
And wisdom's dower the Muses gave,
            Deck ye his grave.

VII. 22.

ANYTE

Anyte of Tegea belongs to the first half of the third century B.C. Twenty-four of her epigrams survive, many of which have been translated by Dr. Garnett and Mr. Gosse. Ep. IX. 144 was intended for inscription upon the base of a statue which stood upon the sea-shore.

'LILIES'

APHRODITE OF THE SEA

THIS is the Cyprian's land, for here she loveth
    to be,
Standing for ever at gaze o'er the gleaming
    waves of the sea ;
Here doth she grant their prayer to sailors
    who crave her grace,
For the waters tremble for dread, so fair is the
    Goddess' face.

IX. 144.

'A RUSTIC OFFERING'

FOR Pan of the shaggy thighs and the nymphs
        who guard the flock,
Here hath Theodotus laid his gift by a lonely
        rock ;
For they stayed him when very weary, in
        summer's parching heat
Their hands poured out a draught and the water
        was honey sweet.

VII. 538.

AN EPITAPH

PROARCHUS, courage slew thee in the fight,
And Pheidias' house is veiled in sorrow's night.
Yet is their epitaph a triumph song
Who die to save the land they love from wrong.

VII. 724.

THE LEVELLER

HE that in life was but a Persian slave
Is great Darius' equal in the grave.

VII. 538.

ASCLEPIADES

Asclepiades, whose emblem is the anemone, belongs to the early part of the third century B.C., and his work is represented by forty poems, of which twenty-eight are in the Erotic Sections. It is now generally agreed that Sicelides (Meleager's Garland, l. 46) was the name given to Asclepiades by the members of the literary circle of Cos, though at one time the name was held to refer to Theocritus. Mr. Mackail appears to assume that the poet was the son of Sicelides, but, so far as I am aware, he is alone in this opinion. The questions that have been raised as to Asclepiades and his associates in this most interesting group are ably discussed by Legrand and Geffchen (see note on Leonidas of Tarentum).

That Meleager should have chosen the most delicate of flowers to be his emblem, whilst Theocritus commends his work as a model of art, should be sufficient comment upon the qualities of Asclepiades' verse, of which too few specimens are included here, but versions of other epigrams will be found in the selections of Wellesley Bland, Merivale, and Mackail. The courtly compliment to Ptolemy's queen (p. 27) contains an idea which has often been repeated, and the same notion was prettily developed by Marot in a huitain which Spenser borrowed :—

DE CUPIDO ET DE SA DAME

Amour trouva celle qui m'est amere,
Et je y estois, j'en sçay bien mieulx le compte :
Bon jour, dict il, bon jour Venus ma mere :
Puis tout à coup il veoit qu'il se mescompte,
Dont la couleur au visage luy monte
D'avoir failly honteux Dieu sçait combien :
Non, non, Amour, ce dy je, n'ayez honte
Plus clers-voyans que vous s'y trompent bien.

CLÉMENT MAROT, 1527.

'ANEMONE'

THE REVELLER TO ZEUS

CAST snow and hail, fold me in darkness' shroud,
Let lightnings blaze, and thunderbolts be hurled,
Unloose the might of every lurid cloud,
Till murky gloom encompass all the world.

For if thou slay me, 'tis the end of all,
Yet if thou leave me life, in spite of ill,
Yea, though a fate more dread than these befall
Love's revel will I keep, undaunted still.

A god doth drive me : in the days of old,
Lord of the world, he mastered even thee ;
'Tis love who taught thee, in a shower of gold,
To pierce the brazen towers of Danäe.

v. 64.

CARPE DIEM

DOST hoard thy maidenhood? small gain is this,
In Hades thou shalt find no lover's kiss ;
Cypris' dear joys are for this life above,
For Death's dull bones and ashes know not
   love.

v. 85.

THE BEST OF ALL

SWEET in summer is snow to him that's athirst,
   and sweet
To sailors when winter is done the Crown of
   the spring to greet.

But this is sweeter than all, and a joy all joys
   above
For lovers, alone together, to sing the praises
   of love.

v. 169.

IN DOUBT

Is this the Cyprian's image, pray,
Or Berenice's ? who shall say
If it resemble more the mien
Of Egypt's or Cythera's Queen ?

XVI. 68.

A MOTTO

SPORTING with sweet Hermione
   I noted that she wore
A broidered girdle, fair to see,
   As ere the Paphian bore.
And round in golden letters ran—
   'Love me, and aye be true ;
But grudge not if another man
   Should love as well as you !'

V. 158.

ON A GROUP OF THE LOVES PLAYING
WITH DICE

NOT two and twenty, yet I tire
   Of Life and all its woe.
Ye Loves why set my heart afire,
   Why will ye vex me so ?
For if I die your sport is o'er,
   Yet doubtless ye would play
At dice for hearts as heretofore,
   Heedless of those ye slay.

XII. 46.

LEONIDAS

Leonidas of Tarentum (about 275 B.C.) was almost certainly a member of the circle to which Asclepiades and Theocritus belonged. Legrand identifies him with Lykidas in Theocritus Id. VII., and considers that Simachidas in the same poem is Theocritus himself. We know from his own poems that Leonidas was poor and expected to die far from his own land, his exile being due probably to the conquests of Pyrrhus in 278 B.C. The latest authorities upon his life and work are Legrand (' Étude sur Théocrite ') Geffchen (' Leonidas von Tarent ') and Mackail ('Five Hundred Epigrams from the Greek Anthology ').

'IVY CLUSTERS'

ON A CHILD

SHE faded ere her time ; her seventh year
    Its course had hardly run
Before she died, and left her comrades here.
    Alas ! poor little one,
Pining because her baby brother died,
    She would not be consoled.

For loveless death has reft him from her side
    Ere he was two years old.
Alas! Peristera, sad ills you bore;
    The Fates work ever thus,
And the worst evils that they have in store
    Are never far from us.

VII. 662.

LIFETIME

LONG ere thou sawest the sun,
Infinite ages had run:
After the daytime is done
    There are infinite years.

Man, what remaineth for thee?
A point too little to see,
Or lesser, if that may be,
    Thy lifetime appears.

Yet evil therein is rife,
It is filled with sorrow and strife;
And sweeter by far than life
    Is the death man fears.

VII. 472 (part only).

'GOING'

'As on her withered prop doth hang the vine,
　　So I upon my staff; and death doth call,
Wilt feign thou hearest not, O soul of mine?
　　And yet, methinks, thy joy of life were small;
To bask in sunshine at hay-harvest tide
　　Three years or four—were that so sweet to
　　　　thee?'
So calmly musing, Gorgus laid aside
　　His life and sought the greater company.

VII. 731.

THE LAST HILL

Go bravely down the road that leadeth thee
　　　　To shadow land;
Straight is the path, it is not hard to see
　　　　And understand;
So gentle the descent, so smooth it lies,
　　　　Thou canst not stray;
And all men go thereon with closed eyes
　　　　Nor miss the way.

App. IV. 39.

ON AN OLD WOMAN

SHE toiled from the early morn, and late her
    slumber came,
But want she held at bay, albeit an ancient
    dame ;
The while she wrought her task and spindle or
    distaff plied,
Crooned she a little song, though age was close
    at her side.
So, busy about the loom, she wrought till the
    dawn was near,
For long is Athenè's course, but the Graces gave
    her cheer ;
As round her aged knees her wrinkled hand
    would wind
A skein of thread for the warp these gave her
    a happy mind.
She saw not the River of Death till eighty years
    had run,
And well had she plied her task e'er the thread
    of her life was spun.

VII. 726.

CALLIMACHUS

Callimachus, whose family came from Cyrene, was keeper of the great Alexandrian library about 260 B.C. In addition to hymns some seventy epigrams by him are still extant, though a few of these are doubtfully authentic. His emblem in the Garland is the sweet myrtle berry, and his work fully justifies the esteem in which he was held by the ancient world—an esteem emphasised by the eulogies of Propertius and Ovid. I have not ventured to translate the lines upon Heraclitus, since the version in ' Ionica,' if not flawless, has become a classic to English readers : both this, and Shakespeare's version of the epigram on Timon (borrowed no doubt from North), are given below.

The epigram upon Theaetetus refers probably to the latter's abandonment of poetry for philosophy : others explain it by supposing that he had made a new departure in dramatic composition which failed to win approval. The fading of the roses in the lover's wreath is discussed by Athenaeus who gives half a dozen possible explanations (Ath. XV. 9).

The epigram on Menoetas' offering recalls one by Mnasalcas which was well translated by Mr. Morley Roberts :—

C

From Promachos to Phoebus, for I yield
　Curved bow and empty quiver unto thee :
　Askest thou arrows? those dire gifts may be
Found in my foemen's hearts upon the field.
　　　　　　　　　　Songs of Energy.

To Heracleitus

They told me, Heracleitus, they told me you
　　were dead ;
They brought me bitter news to hear, and
　　bitter tears to shed ;
I wept as I remembered how often you and I
Had tired the sun with talking and sent him
　　down the sky.
And now that thou art lying, my dear old
　　Carian guest,
A handful of grey ashes long long ago at rest,
Still are thy pleasant voices, thy nightingales,
　　awake,
For Death he taketh all away, but them he
　　cannot take.

　　　　　　　　　　w. cory, *Ionica.*

On Timon

Here lie I, Timon, who alive all living men did
　　hate ;
Pass by and curse thy fill, but pass, and stay
　　not here thy gait.

　　　　　　　　　　SHAKESPEARE.

'*MYRTLE BERRIES*'

TRUE FAME

PURE was the way you chose to tread, you
    seemed to miss renown,
For that fair path shall never lead to Bacchus'
    ivied crown;
And yet the names that heralds hail may live
    their little day,
Whilst Hellas gives you wisdom's wreath that
    shall not fade away.

IX. 565.

' DETECTED '

OUR friend was wounded, and we never knew !
Yet marked you not the laboured breath he
    drew ?
And as he quaffed his cup—'twas but the third—
I saw the petals of his roses stirred
And scattered on the ground, a certain sign
Of Eros' flame ; no random guess is mine.
Full well I see the way that love has run ;
A thief myself, I know the tracks of one.

XII. 134.

'LOVE AND SPORT'

As o'er the hill the hunters go
To track the slot of hind or hare,
Despite the hoar-frost and the snow,
If any say 'The beast is there'
They scorn to take her in the lair.
And lo, my heart is e'en as they :
It ever seeks the flying fair,
But passes by an easy prey.

XII. 102.

AN OFFERING

MENOETAS' quiver, with his bow,
    Serapis, at thy feet doth lie.
No shafts are here—the stricken foe
    Of Hesperis shall tell thee why.

XIII. 7.

ASLEEP

SAON, the son of Dicon, here doth lie
In holy sleep : say not the good can die.

VII. 451.

THE LOST PLAYMATE

CRETHIS, the Samian maidens are sadly seek-
    ing you,
Loving the tales you often told, the pretty games
    you knew.
Sweetest of all their comrades, your voice was
    ever dear,
But now you sleep the endless sleep, and these
    shall join you here.

VII. 459.

ON A CENOTAPH

WOULD there had never been a ship to run
        The hazard of the deep :
We had not wept for Diocleides' son
        As vainly now we weep.
Dead in the dreary waste, dear Sopolis,
        You drift upon the wave,
And nought is left us but your name, and this
        Only an empty grave.

VII. 271.

NOSSIS

Nossis, to whom Meleager assigns the scented flag, belongs probably to the third century B.C., and if the epitaph upon Rhintho of Syracuse was written soon after the death of the comedian to whom it refers, the writer would be about contemporary with Leonidas of Tarentum.

Her work is represented by twelve poems in the Anthology, and as Meleager speaks of her as ' She on whose tablets love did melt the wax,' we may presume that some of her love poems have been lost.

One surviving epigram gives such fragments of information as we possess about her life, and runs thus—' If thou sail to fair Mitylene to gather Sappho's love flowers, say that I was accepted of the Muses and the land of Locri bore me.'

Rhintho, the inventor of a kind of burlesque, flourished about 300 B.C., and is sometimes called ' of Tarentum,' because he settled in that city early in the third century.

'SCENTED FLAGS

TO EROS

EROS, sweetest of all ! there is naught is lovely
    beside thee,
  Nay, to the savour of love, honey is bitter to
    me.
Thus saith Nossis to man, ' If Cypris her kiss
    hath denied thee,
  Then are the roses of life hidden for ever
    from thee.'

v. 170.

EPITAPH UPON RHINTHO

SMILE gaily as you pass me by,
    And give a friendly hail,
Rhintho of Syracuse am I,
    A little nightingale ;
One whom the Muses have not spurned,
    For all my twittering tone,
For by mock-tragedy I earned
    An ivy of my own.

VII. 414.

POSIDIPPUS

Posidippus may be the well-known writer of Comedy who began to exhibit in 289 B.C. Twenty-six epigrams are extant under his name, of which all but six occur in the Anthology.

It is, however, possible that the epigrammatist is not identical with the new Comedy writer, but belongs to a rather later date, though there is no certain evidence on this point.

Doricha, the subject of the poem on p. 42, was by tradition the mistress of Charaxus, Sappho's brother; the ' white ode ' by the wonderful Lesbian which mentioned her is lost, having been destroyed through the bigotry of a prurient-minded age; and the town of Naucratis ceased to be of any importance with the rise of Alexandria. The readings in line five of this epigram are doubt-ful. One of the best known of Posidippus' poems is that imitated by Bacon (' The world 's a bubble '), but a better version of this with the answer by Metrodorus is given below.

From Posidippus

What course of life should wretched mortals
    take?
In courts hard questions large contention
    make:

Care dwells in houses, labour in the field :
Tumultuous seas affrighting dangers yield :
In foreign lands thou never canst be blest :
If rich thou art in fear, if poor distrest ;
In wedlock frequent discontentments swell,
Unmarried persons as in deserts dwell :
How many troubles are with children born ?
Yet he that wants them counts himself forlorn !
Young men are wanton, and of wisdom void,
Grey hairs are cold, unfit to be employed.
Who would not one of these two offers choose,
Not to be born, or breath with speed to lose.

SIR JOHN BEAUMONT.

From Metrodorus

In every way of life true pleasure flows,
Immortal fame from public action grows,
Within the doors is found appeasing rest,
In fields the gifts of nature are exprest.
The sea brings gain, the rich abroad provide
To blaze their names, the poor their wants to
    hide ;
All households best are governed by a wife,
His cares are light who bears a single life,
Sweet children are delights which Marriage
    bless,
He that hath none disturbs his thoughts the
    less.
Strong youth can triumph in victorious deeds,
Old age the soul with pious notions feeds,
All states are good, and they are falsely led
Who wish to be unborn, or quickly dead.

SIR JOHN BEAUMONT
(1582-1628).

'WILD FLOWERS FROM THE CORN'

AN IMMORTAL

YOUR beauty long ago is dust, and dust your
    lovely hair,
Your ribbons and the scented robe that once
    you loved to wear,
You flung it round Charaxus, and held him to
    your heart,
That night you spent in rapture, till morning
    bade you part.
But still in Sappho's flawless ode is your beloved
    name,
And lives for ever in a song oblivion cannot
    claim ;
So men must love you, Doricha, while Nau-
    cratis shall be,
Or ships shall stir the long lagoons where
    Nilus meets the sea.

App. III. 77.

LOVE'S ARMOURY

THE little loves espied the dainty maid,
    Irenion (for she strayed
Near to a golden bower where Cypris lay),
    And forth they winged their way

To mark her beauty—never purest flower
      Had so divine a dower,
Nor sculptor's art could match her as she
    stood
      Decked in sweet maidenhood.
Then stole those wantons many winged darts
      Wherewith to pierce men's hearts,
And now his purple bowstring Eros arms
      With fair Irenion's charms.

                  v. 194.

RHIANUS

Rhianus of Bena in Crete, who is represented by marjoram in Meleager's Garland, flourished about 200 B.C., or perhaps rather earlier. He was master of the Palaestra and distinguished as a poet and grammarian, but most of his work seems to have been of a more solid character than that contained in the Anthology and consisted chiefly of metrical histories of various cities.

According to Suetonius, the Emperor Tiberius thought so highly of his style that he ordered the poet's bust to be placed in the public libraries. Ten of his epigrams are still extant.

'MARJORAM'

THE PRUDENT LOVER

ONCE as you chanced to stray
Along a narrow way
The Graces met you,
And then the lovely three
Methinks did all agree
There to beset you.

With fingers rosy-fair
Closely they held you there
In sweet embraces,
And in that happy hour
You gained the lovely dower
Of all the graces.

And since so fair you are
I greet you, from afar,
Danger discerning ;
My dear, it is not well
To set dry asphodel
Where fire is burning.

XII. 121.

ALCAEUS

Alcaeus of Messene, the author of twenty-two poems in the Anthology, is represented in Meleager's Garland by the hyacinth, which is there called ' the flower that cries aloud,' because the marks upon the leaves were supposed to represent ἀί, ἀί. Some of the epigrams are headed Alcaeus of Mytilene, but this is beyond a doubt a mistake, and no work of the great lyric poet survives in the Palatine MS.

The Alcaeus of the Anthology flourished at the end of the third and beginning of the second centuries B.C., and several of his poems refer to historical events which took place between 218 and 191 B.C.

In the second of the two epigrams here translated the reference to Athene is due to the legend that the goddess rejected the flute in disgust at the undignified attitude which its use entailed.

'HYACINTH'

THE HUNTER OF MEN

I HATE the god of love, for brutes
　　Alone should feel his dart,
And yet for wantonness he shoots
　　His arrows at my heart.

No god I wot should torture me
   To sate a cruel whim ;
And though my soul his captive be,
   How should it profit him ?

V. 10.

ON A STATUE OF MARSYAS

No longer through the Phrygian pines your
   melodies may float,
No longer from the pierced flute may sound
   your magic note :
Touched by your hand Athene's reed flowered
   into song of yore,
Those flowers, O nymph-born Marsyas, shall
   blossom never more.
Your hands are bound in fetters now ; to
   Phoebus you atone,
Because against immortal skill you dared to set
   your own ;
And though your flute was honey sweet as e'en
   his harp could be,
Yet Death was all the prize you won, your
   Crown of victory.

XVI. 8.

DIOSCORIDES

Dioscorides, to whom Meleager assigns the Muses' cyclamen (or spice plant?), belongs to the end of the third or beginning of the second century, and by some commentators is identified with a philosopher mentioned by Diogenes Laertius.

About forty epigrams assigned to him are extant, half of which are epitaphs, and that here translated is one of several dealing with the kindly relation of master to slave. The Lydians were regarded as the lowest type of slave, but this one seems to have been ' paedagogus ' to his young master and his name was Timanthes. In an anonymous epitaph of the same character, a Persian promises fidelity in the nether world. This epigram of Dioscorides has been paraphrased in ' Ionica.'

' CYCLAMEN '

' WAITING '

I WAS a Lydian slave, and yet an honoured
    grave
        Worthy the free,
Dear lord and foster-son, for loving service done
        You gave to me.

Live long in happiness, far from all pain and
    stress,
        Untouched of ill :
Then come at last to me ; in Hades I will be
        Your servant still.

VII. 178.

TO ATHENION SINGING

YOU sung the steed and Ilion doomed,
As waves of flame did o'er her roll,
And as you sung the fire consumed
        My very soul.
She bore ten years of toil and strife,
For scarce an hour could I endure,
But as you told her death my life
        Was mine no more.

V. 138.

DIONYSIUS

There were several writers of this name, and it is not possible to determine whether all the fourteen epigrams in the Anthology are by one hand or by several ; but Dionysius of Cyzicus, the author of the first epigram here translated, presumably flourished about 190 B.C., since the Eratosthenes whom it commemorates died in 197 at the age of eighty-two.

The second is headed ' Dionysius the Sophist,' and may be the work of another writer.

EUTHANASIA

No dulling sickness fell to dim your light,
    Softly the kind years crept,
And lulled you for the inevitable night ;
    And so you slept.

O Eratosthenes, 'twas yours to win
    In life fair thoughts and high,
And though you sleep far from the land wherein
    Your fathers lie.

Yet what of that? since loving thought can reach
    Where'er your grave may be,
Though in a stranger's land, where Proteus'
    beach
    Doth bound the sea.

VII. 78.

ROSA ROSARUM

WHICH roses do you offer me,
These on your cheek, or those beside you?
Since both are passing fair to see,
Which roses do you offer me?
To give me both would you agree,
Or must I choose, and so divide you?
Which roses do you offer me,
These on your cheek, or those beside you?

V. 81.

DAMAGETUS

Damagetus, the poet of the ' dark violet,' belongs to the second century B.C., or the end of the third ; there are twelve epigrams by him in the Anthology, of which all except three are epitaphs.

The name of ' Theopompus' son ' in the epitaph here translated is uncertain, being given both as Ariemenes and Aristagoras, for the lines occur twice in the Palatine MS.

'PURPLE VIOLETS'

A DORIAN EPITAPH

SERVING Ambracia his death he won,
    For her he raised the shield,
And this the choice of Theopompus' son,
    Rather to die than yield.
No marvel this, for he was Dorian born;
    Wherefore in very truth,
So he might serve his land, he thought it scorn
    To care for life and youth.

VII. 231.

ANTIPATER OF SIDON

Antipater of Sidon, who flourished during the last half of the second century B.C., is often confused with his namesake of Thessalonica (p. 84). According to Jacobs about ninety epigrams belong to the former, and these are amongst the most interesting in the Anthology, not only for their skill and subtlety of touch, but because of the admirable criticism contained in some of them. Thus he speaks of Pindar as ' The trumpet of Pieria who forged the bronze of hallowed hymns,' and calls Sappho ' the fosterling of Cypris and Eros with whose aid Persuasion wove a wreath of song that lives for ever.' Of so high a quality is his work that Professor Murray places him next to, and not far below, Meleager ; perhaps even the few versions here given may serve to show his versatility.

The first of these epigrams helps to fix the poet's date, for Corinth was destroyed in 146 B.C. ; more direct evidence is afforded by the ' De Oratore' of Cicero.

The dedicatory epigram on p. 57 was intended to accompany an offering made to Athene Ergane, the goddess of the wool-workers, by Telesilla, the daughter of Diocles.

'*PHŒNICIAN CYPRESS*'

PLEUREZ DOUX ALCYONS

O CORINTH, Dorian Corinth, where is thy
    beauty now?
So fair it was, and where the crown that shone
    upon thy brow?
A coronet of towers and countless wealth was
    thine,
With many a noble palace, and many an holy
    shrine.
What of thy myriad warriors, thy dames of
    high estate?
O daughter of a thousand woes, thy place is
    desolate!
Nay, thou hast left no footprint that future
    men may say
' Here Corinth stood!'—the tide of war hath
    swept them all away.
Yet we the deathless Nereids, the halcyons of
    thy sea,
In loneliness are faithful yet to wail thy woe
    for thee.

                    IX. 151.

ON HOMER'S BUST

THE seer of the Blessed Gods, the herald of
     heroes' might,
  Like to another sun on the life of Hellas
     was he ;
The ageless voice of the world, and the Muses'
     deathless light,
  Though he be still and hid 'neath the brine-
     washed sand of the sea.

VII. 6.

ON A DEAD PLANE

A WITHERED trunk am I, but lapped around me
     Behold a clinging vine.
See how her living loveliness hath crowned me,
     Making her beauty mine.
Of old I spread a fostering shade above her,
     To guard her tender fruit,
When I was fair as she, my faithful lover,
     With grace of leaf and shoot ;
So be it yours a woman's heart to cherish,
     One that is dear and true,
To answer love with love that shall not perish,
     Though death should sunder you.

IX. 231.

A DRINKING SONG

THOUGH storm winds may rage when the
    Pleiads are low,
And tempests may roar, yet no terrors I know;
The waters may crash on the rocks by the sea;
The lightnings may flash, and not terrify me.
But the drinker of water's the terror I dread,
Who recalls every word that the toper hath
    said.

XI. 31.

DROWNED IN HARBOUR

EVERY sea is the sea; and the Cyclades are
    not to blame.
Vainly hath Helle's race, and the Needles their
    evil fame;
These I escaped unscathed, and I deemed that
    my peril was past,
For in Scarphé's haven I lay, but there she
    whelmed me at last.
Pray for a safe return who will, but take warning
    from me,
Lo, I cry from my grave, ' The sea shall be ever
    the sea.'

VII. 639.

A SHORT LIFE AND A MERRY

SHORT lived am I, Seleucus, so astrologers
    declare,
And well I wot it must be so, but wherefore
    should I care?
The downward way is one for all—if fast my
    course must be,
The sooner shall I know the doom that Minos
    gives to me.
Good wine's the horse for life's high road;
    come, let us drink, my friend,
While others slink by devious ways—they'll
    meet us in the end.

XI. 23.

AN OFFERING

THE shuttle that sang at morn when the earliest
    swallow cries,
Flitting through Pallas' loom as swift as the
    halcyon flies,
And the whirling spindle of mine that, spite of
    its heavy head,
Swiftly would twirl and turn, spinning the twisted
    thread:

With these are my bobbins laid, and their friend
    the plaited creel,
That guarded the distaff's work and held the
    thread and the reel.
These give I, the tools of my craft, and I loved
    to toil therein ;
Be mindful of Telesilla, O goddess of them that
    spin.

                          VI. 160.

HERMODORUS

Nothing is known certainly of this writer, but the ' Syrian nard,' assigned to him by Meleager, may be an indication of his native country.

The epigram here translated is the only one ascribed to Hermodorus in the Anthology as we possess it, and even this occurs in Planudes only, being thus one of the indications that the Palatine MS. is incomplete. The statues referred to are the Cnidian Aphrodite of Praxiteles, and the Athene of Pheidias.

' NARD '

THE STATUES OF APHRODITE AND PALLAS

HAPLY if thou hast seen Cythera's lovely queen
        In Cnidos' land,
' No marvel,' thou didst say, ' that gods and men obey
        Her least command.'
And yet if thou draw near to Pallas of the spear
        In Cecrop's town,
So wondrous fair is she, Paris shall seem to thee
        A very clown.

XVI. 170.

MELEAGER

The little we know as to the life of the compiler of the Greek Anthology is derived chiefly from his own verses. He was born at Gadara in Palestine, educated at Tyre, and lived the latter part of his life in Cos, where he died at an advanced age. These few facts, together with his father's name Eucrates, are set forth in the epigram translated on p. 77. There is no doubt that the poet flourished during the first century B.C., and the scholiast gives his date as during the reign of the last Seleucus, 95-93 B.C. His epigrams number in all 154, of which the majority are on the subject of love in one aspect or another; two are epitaphs upon himself, and fifteen more are found in the section devoted to Sepulchral verses. Almost all these compositions are in elegiac verse, but the ode on Spring is a notable exception, being in hexameters, and is on that account excluded from most selections. Much has been written as to Meleager's style and merits as a poet, the criticisms varying between that of Lord Chesterfield, who advises his son that none of the writers in the Anthology are worthy of study or to be compared with Martial, and that of Mr. Herbert Paul, who represents Meleager as being like

Swinburne at his best.   Perhaps neither judgment is altogether justified, and the reader who has no Greek may form his own opinion by reading Dr. Headlam's ' Fifty Poems of Meleager.'

The idea of ' The Truant Love ' (p. 63) seems to be borrowed from Moschus whose ode on ' Love the Runaway ' was imitated by Ben Jonson, La Fontaine in 'Psyche,' and Spenser in the ' Fairy Queen.'

' Love's Torment' (p. 66) represents part only of the original, but there is authority for treating this portion as a separate poem.

The epigram on p. 75 is often quoted as the original of Ben Jonson's ' Drink to me only with thine eyes,' which, however, is really a literal translation from Philostratus.

The epitaph upon Heliodora is very difficult to translate.   Dr. Hawtrey's version in elegiacs comes nearer to the original text than most translations, and I therefore quote it, but Mr. Lang's paraphrase (' Tears for my lady dead') appears to me to be nearer the spirit of the Greek.

To Heliodora

Though the earth hide thee, yet there, even
there, my Heliodora,
All that is left I give, tears of my love to thy
grave.
Tears how bitterly shed on thy tomb bedewed
by my weeping,
Pledge of my fond regret, pledge of affection
for thee.

Piteously, piteously still, but in vain grieves on
    Meleager :
Thou art among the dead : Acheron heeds
    not my woe.
Where is the flower that I loved?   Death has
    torn it away in the springtide,
Torn it away, and the dust stains the fair
    leaves in their bloom.
Genial earth, be it thine, at the mourner's
    humble entreaty,
Gently to hold in thine arms her whom I
    ever deplore.

DR. E. C. HAWTREY.

'WHITE VIOLETS'

'LOVE AT BALL'

THE Love that dwells within me knows
    Full well the player's art,
And, Heliodora, now he throws
    To you my fluttering heart.

Send forth your Love to share the play,
    'Twere wanton to refuse ;
But if you toss my heart away,
    You break the rules and lose.

V. 214.

'OYEZ'

THE truant Love! hath any eye descried him?
At dawn he left his bed, and forth did fare;
Mark his bold words and mien, his mock
    despair,
His wanton laugh, his wings, the shafts beside
    him.
Who was his sire?   The winds have all denied
    him,
And neither earth nor sea will own for heir
                The truant, Love.

So give good heed, for all things fear and chide
    him,
Lest for your souls he lay a deadly snare.
Ah! there he is—now have I found his lair,
For, lurking in my lady's eyes, I spied him,
                The truant, Love.

                    v. 177.

'THE CAPTIVE'

Now a captive Love lies,
Though he thought him secure ;
And though swiftly he flies,
Now a captive Love lies,
For he saw your bright eyes,
And he stooped to the lure :
Now a captive Love lies,
Though he thought him secure.

XII. 113

SURRENDER

Prostrate I lie, set foot on me,
    Ah cruel god, I vow
However sore the burden be,
    I 'm schooled to bear it now.

Thy burning arrows well I know,
    Yet all these brands are vain
My heart is ashes long ago,
    And cannot glow again.

XII. 48

A LOVER'S COMPLAINT

THE beating of the wings of Love is ever in
    mine ears,
Sweet sorrow brings to dear desire her gift of
    silent tears,
Oblivion comes not night or day since Eros'
    magic spell
Hath graved upon my inmost heart the form I
    love so well.
Ye winged sprites, ye little Loves, ah tell me this,
    I pray,
Why gat ye skill to come to me but none to fly
    away?

V. 212.

AT DAWN

O MORNING star, I bid farewell to thee,
    Thou herald of the day;
Come back as silent Hesper bringing me
    Her whom you take away.

XII. 114.

E

LOVE'S TORMENT

O SUFFERING soul, thou burnest in the fire
And now revivest, catching breath again.
Yet wherefore weep? 'tis idle to complain ;
When thou didst nurture love, that torment dire,
Didst thou not know he giveth grief for hire?
Didst thou not know his fairest wage is pain,
                                    O suffering soul?

Chill of his frost, and torture of his pyre,
Thyself hast chosen these that are thy bane.
Just meed for service done shalt thou obtain,
Scorched by the burning honey of desire,
                                    O suffering soul !

XII. 132 (part only).

THE GAMBLER

LOVE always was a little rake.
E'en as on Cypris' breast he lay
His baby hands the dice would take,
Love always was a little rake.
One morn he made my soul the stake,
And now he 's gambled it away.
Love always was a little rake,
E'en as on Cypris' breast he lay.

XII. 47.

THE MESSAGE

DORCAS ! go and tell her this—
　Run, and mind you say it twice
Lest a word she chance to miss :
　Hurry ! stop ! repeat it thrice.
Fly, you sluggard, don't forget :
　Dorcas ! why so quick away ?
Fool ! you haven't heard as yet
　Half of what I want to say.
Dorcas, add to what I said—
　No, again I 'm blundering,
Leave that out, and say instead—
　Nothing—no, say everything !
Don't omit a single word ;
　I 'm the fool to trust in you.
Wherefore hurry ? it 's absurd—
　Can't you see I 'm coming too.

v. 182.

SWEET AND BITTER

HONEY drinker ! wherefore seek
Heliodora's dainty cheek ?
Lo, the spring has opened fair
Cups of nectar everywhere.

'She is sweet,' you seem to say,
'Sweeter than the flowers of May:
Yet beware in gathering,
Love, like me, will surely sting.'
So I think you preach to me,
Silly lover-loving bee.
Get you gone—for long ago
Well I knew 'twas ever so!

v. 163.

LOVE'S ARROWS

NAY, by Demo's locks of gold,
    Heliodora's pretty feet,
By the scented bowers that hold
    Dainty Timo, fair and sweet;
Nay, by Anticleia's eyes,
    And her smile that courts caresses
By the dewy wreath that lies
    On my Dorothea's tresses,
Vainly now your bow you bend,
    Gone is every winged dart.
Foolish Eros, thus to spend
    All your arrows on my heart.

v. 198.

LOVE'S FIRE

SEEING my love at noon upon the way,
When to the reaper Summer bows her head,
I felt the burning of a two-fold ray,
This from Love's eyes, and that by Phoebus
    shed :
Night quenched the one, the fiercer flame hath
    spread,
Fanned by the beauty that in dreams I see ;
So sleep, the healer, brings new pain to me,
And in my soul Love's living fire hath fed.

XII. 127.

LOVE IN A STORM

LIKE some frail boat amid the storms of spring,
My heart is tossed upon Love's troubled sea ;
Now fall your tears as rain, now gladdening,
Your sunny glances clear the sky for me :
Mid blinding waves my helpless course must be,
By tempests rocked my barque doth reel and
    swing :
Make me some signal, or of love or hate
Whereby to steer, or see at least my fate.

XII. 156.

LOVE AT AUCTION

'LOVE is for sale!' and not a whit care I
That on his mother's breast asleep he lie;
For what avails it such a knave to keep,
So pert of mien, who, laughing, feigns to weep?
Swift are his hands to wound, his wings to fly;
Shameless he is, a babbler, and a spy,
Even his mother knows his cruelty;
A most unnatural rogue—I'll sell him cheap,
                        'Love is for sale!

If any merchant outward bound will buy,
Here is the boy—but stay!   I heard him sigh,
And piteous tears his pretty eyelids steep.
Poor child! be comforted, for if you creep
Close to my darling's heart, I will not cry—
                        'Love is for sale!
                                v. 178.

EROS CRYING

ROBBER of hearts, you are weeping there,
    Reft of your arrows and cruel bow;
Where are the pinions that clove the air
    As oars may cleave through the waves
        below?

Beauty's glances have wrought your woe,
  Burning arrows that scorch nor spare.
Suffering Eros, you made them so,
  Now it is yours our pain to share.

                                    XII. 144.

TO EROS

A CURSE is Love, a curse—and yet 'tis vain
  So to cry out on him with tear and sigh;
The wanton only laughs if we complain.
  Chide him, he laughs the more to hear our
      cry ;
Revile him, and he seems to thrive thereby ;
  And yet, O Cypris, daughter of the sea,
Methinks the course of nature is awry,
  That such a firebrand should be born of
    Thee.

                                    V. 176.

LOVE'S PEDIGREE

  IF Love, the bane of mortal hearts,
  Is ever armed with fiery darts,
  And if he laugh in angry wise,
  Or mock our pain with shameless eyes,
  It is not strange : the Lord of arms
  Was stricken by his mother's charms ;

And she that calls Hephaestus lord,
Is queen alike of flame and sword ;
Yea, and her mother was the wave,
She that for wrath doth storm and rave
When lashing winds her anger stir—
And this the boy hath learned of her.
Unknown his father's race and name,
But not on him doth lie the blame.
These baneful gifts are from the three,
Hephaestus, Ares, and the sea.

v. 180.

SPRING

STILLED is winter's gusty breath,
Now the spring awakeneth ;
See, she brings the blushing hours
Gay with laughter, glad with flowers,
And the sombre earth is seen
Robed in bravery of green,
While the teeming branches bear
Opening buds to deck her hair.
Nurtured by the dews of morn
Many a tender bloom is born,
And the meadows laugh and sing,
For the rose is opening.

Blithe of heart the shepherd swain
Tunes the merry pipe again,
While upon the mountain steep
Browse his goats and woolly sheep.
Gladly doth the mariner
Feel the gentle zephyr stir ;
Safely now his keel may glide
O'er the waste of waters wide.
Dionysus now to thee
Mortals sing thine Evöe ;
Sound we thus the Vine-god's praise,
Crowned with clustered ivy sprays.
Now the bees in busy train
Ply their cunning art again ;
Ceaseless in the hive they toil,
Labouring with the new-won spoil,
Building up the waxen comb
In their myriad-chambered home.
Now the tuneful choir of air
Makes us music everywhere.
On the wave the halcyon,
By the sedgy stream the swan,
Round about the eaves the swallow,
Nightingales in every hollow
Tell the coming of the spring ;
Thus rejoices everything.
If gay raiment deck the earth,

And the shepherd pipe for mirth,
While the fleecy flock and herd,
Swarming bee and singing bird,
So in gladness all agree ;
If the sailor trust the sea,
And the god of wine and youth
Lead the dance, in very sooth,
Can the bard from song refrain
Now the spring has come again ?

IX. 363.

TO ZENOPHILA SLEEPING

As there my dainty lady lies,
I would I were a god of sleep,
A wingless one, my watch to keep
Above her closèd eyes.

None should be near, not even he
Whose magic Zeus himself doth own
For I would guard her, I alone,
And fold her close to me.

V. 174.

THE LOVER'S WREATH

VIOLETS white and daffodillies,
I will twine with laughing lilies,
Sprays of myrtle, and withal
Crocus sweet and virginal.
Here the blue-bell's purple glows
With the lover-loving rose,
Meet for Heliodore to wear
'Mid the love-locks of her hair.
Go, on my beloved's head,
Happy wreath, your petals shed.

v. 147.

ON A DRINKING CUP

THE goblet's boast is this
To know a perfect bliss
   All joys above,
Whenas the wine she sips
To touch the honeyed lips
   Of my fair love.
Would she but lay on mine
Those lips she sets to thine,
   Thou envied bowl,
Ah that my love would deign
With one long kiss to drain
   My very soul !

v. 171.

TO HIS DEAD LOVER

TEARS are my gift though the piled earth
      above
            Your grave doth hide you,
All other offering save the lees of love
            Hath Death denied you.
Tears of a broken heart, endless lament
            Your tomb to cover,
For your libation and your monument,
            Dear friend and lover.
'Pity, ah, Pity,' Meleager cries,
            Lone and forsaken,
So dear is she, and Acheron will despise
            Her he hath taken.
His hand hath reft my very soul's desire ;
            The flower I cherished,
Torn from my heart and sullied in the mire,
            Her beauty perished.
Dear Earth, we all are nurtured at thy breast,
            Hear thou my weeping ;
O Mother, lull her gently, let her rest
            Safe in thy keeping.

                          VII. 476.

MELEAGER'S EPITAPH

O STRANGER, lightly tread
Above the tomb, where, with the holy dead,
   I sleep, a long life past,
For rest, the meed of all, is mine at last.

   'Tis Meleager's grave,
The son of Eucrates, the Muses' slave,
   And the glad Graces' praise
With Love's sweet tears were woven in my
   lays.

   A nurture fair was mine
In holy Gadara and Tyre divine,
   But this Meropian isle
Gladdened mine age with her beloved smile.

   To Syrians 'Peace' I say,
And greet the Tyrian in his native way;
   But if a Greek thou be,
I say 'Farewell'; say thou the same to me.
                        VII. 419.

PHILODEMUS

Philodemus of Gadara belongs to the first century B.C., but must have been later than Meleager, who would have mentioned so distinguished a fellow-citizen had they been contemporaries. He was a well-known figure in Roman society, being a friend of Piso, Consul in 58 B.C., in connection with whom Cicero speaks of him with respect and esteem. Horace also mentions him in Sat. 1. 2. 121, though some critics hold, on insufficient grounds, that the passage refers to another Philodemus. He wrote upon philosophical subjects, and seems to have professed the Epicurean system.

Of the thirty-six epigrams in the Anthology which are credited to him four are probably spurious, and about half the remainder are love poems. The former of the two here translated is suspected by Jacobs to be by Meleager, partly on account of the style, but also because the name Heliodora is a favourite with the earlier Gadarene poet. Both Cepalas and Planudes attribute it to Philodemus, though this evidence is not conclusive.

A TRAITOR

My boding soul doth say,
' Be warned and flee away,
   My wisdom borrow.
What earned I heretofore
From loving Heliodore
   But tears and sorrow?'

O traitor soul, 'tis vain
The wisdom that you feign
   Your guile to cover,
Knowing I cannot flee;
For while you monish me,
   'Tis *you* that love her.

V. 24.

'CONSTANCY'

My dainty queen's a sweet brunette
   With softly curling tresses,
Her cheek than down is tenderer yet,
   Her words are like caresses.

Hers is a voice whose gentle tone
  Doth breathe a spell as mighty
As that from the enchanted zone
  That girdles Aphrodite.

Her love she gives, nor asks reward,
  And ne'er will I forget her,
O Cypris bright my vow record—
  Till I shall find a better !

V. 121

CRINAGORAS

*Crinagoras of Mitylene, of whose epigrams
fifty are extant, lived during the reign of Augustus
at Rome. Many of his poems are upon public
events and well-known persons in Roman society,
but he is one of the most graceful and pleasant
of all the writers of minor verse. The epigram
below, which was sent with a gift of roses to a
bride who was to be married on the day after her
birthday, is said to have been addressed to Antonia,
who married Drusus.*

WINTER ROSES

WE roses once were fain
To wait till Spring should reign,
  But now we waken,
Despite the winter snow,
With blushing hearts aglow,
  Our wont forsaken.
We greet with smiles and mirth
This day that marked your birth,
  The winter scorning,

F

For when its course is run
Comes with to-morrow's sun
    Your wedding morning :
And so that we be seen,
Chosen of beauty's queen
    To deck her tresses,
We count our happy fate
Sweeter than theirs who wait
    The sun's caresses.

VI. 345.

DEATH IN A FOREIGN LAND

ALAS that we, with idle hope our guide,
        Should wander far,
Forgetting baneful death is near our side
        That hope to mar.
Was not Seleucus in his words and ways
        A blameless one ?
And yet he died before his youthful days
        Their course had run.
In the Iberian land, 'neath alien skies,
        His grave is lone;
And far—so far—from Lesbos there he lies
        On shores unknown.

VII. 376.

A PRAYER

POSEIDON, shaker of the earth, be kind
To others too that cross the Aegean Sea,
Thou who didst guard me from the Thracian
    wind,
Safe to the haven where I fain would be.

                x. 24.

ANTIPATER OF THESSALONICA

Antipater of Thessalonica, the author of rather over one hundred epigrams, flourished at about the beginning of our era. He was appointed Governor of Thessalonica by his friend Piso, Consul in 15 B.C.

Many of his epigrams are interesting for their historical allusions, as, for example, those on the battle of Actium, and Germanicus' eastern expedition.

The little poem here translated has a close parallel in Ovid, Amores, I. XIII. 17.

A RONDEAU

Now Dawn is come, Chrysilla ; long ago
  I heard the clarion note of chanticleer,
  Who brings the envious dawn-lady near.
Foul fall thee, evil bird, my churlish foe,
Who drivest me from home and love, although
  I hate the busy babble I must hear,
               Now Dawn is come.

Hath age, Tithonus, chilled the generous glow
   Of youth? is Eos' kiss no longer dear,
     That, all too soon, thou biddest day appear?
For thou hast sent thy partner forth—and lo
          Now Dawn is come.

                 v. 3.

ARCHIAS

Archias has been identified with Cicero's friend in whose defence one of the orations was delivered ; this identification is, however, doubtful. The Anthology contains forty-one epigrams under this name, but these may be by several hands ; and that here translated probably belongs to the first century A.D.

INELUCTABILE

WHY counsel me from Love to flee ?
I cannot thus escape disaster ;
Nay, since a wingèd God is he,
Why counsel me from Love to flee ?
However light my foot should be
His tireless wings would follow faster ;
Why counsel me from Love to flee ?
I cannot thus escape disaster !

v. 59.

BIANOR

Bianor was a native of Bithynia, and lived during the reign of Tiberius (A.D. 14-37).

'THE CROWN OF LIFE'

'THE meanest slave beneath the sun,
None is too low to rank above him.'
Ah yes, and yet the wretch you shun,
The meanest slave beneath the sun,
Is master of the soul of one,
For he has found a heart to love him.

XI. 364.

THYMOCLES

Thymocles is represented by one epigram only.
His date is unknown.

'TIME FLIETH AND NEVER CLAPS
HIS WINGS'

HAPLY you now recall the word that I spoke ;
    'twas sooth,
That the fairest and fleetest of all is the hour of
    the prime of youth.
Not the swiftest bird of the air may catch that
    hour that is fled :
See now, your flowers, that were fair, all fallen
    to earth and dead.

XII. 32.

ALPHEUS

Alpheus of Mitylene has twelve epigrams assigned to him, and as one of these occurs in Strato's collection there is some reason to believe that he lived in or before the reign of Hadrian.

The epigram upon the sleeping Eros does not occur in the Palatine MS.

ON A SLEEPING EROS

Now Love is sleeping, from his hand
I 'll steal away his burning brand,
And from his shoulder will I dare
To take the quiver hanging there.
For tho' he sleep, and stricken hearts
Have respite from his fiery darts
And rest perchance a little while,
Yet still I fear his wanton guile,
Lest in a vision he should see
Some new device for wounding me.
So full of craft is he, I know
His very dreams may work me woe.

XVI. 212.

ANTIPHILUS

Antiphilus of Byzantium is the author of fifty-two epigrams, of which three are doubtful. That he was writing in the middle of the first century A.D. is made clear by his mention of the restoration of liberty to Rhodes in the year 53.

'TO-MORROW'

NEAR to my home I said, 'To-morrow's sun
Shall surely see my weary voyage done.'
    But Ocean was my grave, and e'er the word
Died on my lips my course in life was run.

And since a little word brought death to me,
Say not 'To-morrow this or that shall be.'
    For not the lightest whisper goes unheard,
And Nemesis shall have her will of thee.

VII. 630.

JULIUS POLYAENUS

Julius Polyaenus is the author of three epigrams only, and is supposed to be identical with one C. Julius Polyaenus, a duumvir of Corinth under Nero, and the conclusion that he was a native of Corcyra is supported by the reference to Scheria (another name for that island) in the prayer here translated.

A PRAYER

O ZEUS, thine ears are filled with many voices;
    For thou dost ever hear
Their grateful praise whom hope fulfilled re-
  joices,
    And prayers of trembling fear.
Yet now from Scheria's plain, thy holy dwelling,
    Hearing my prayer to thee,
Send forth thy word inviolate, foretelling
    A safe return to me,
That so to-day may end mine exile dreary,
    That I no longer roam;
The years of wandering have left me weary,
    And I would be at home.

IX. 7.

MYRINUS

Myrinus probably belongs to the first century of our era, but there are no means of fixing his date accurately, and only four of his epigrams are extant.   To Secundus the same remarks apply.

LOVE IN DANGER

YE Nymphs, 'tis Thyrsis herds your sheep,
  The swain who pipes so fairly ;
Not Pan, who haunts the mountain steep,
  Can tune the reed more rarely.

But now he sleeps—a shady nook
  And noontide thirst bedrouse him—
So Love hath taken Thyrsis' crook
  Until the shepherd rouse him.

Haste, Nymphs ! awake your herdsman bold,
  Lest, ere his slumber ceases,
Some prowling wolf attack the fold
  And Love be torn in pieces.

                                    VII. 703.

SECUNDUS

See under Myrinus, p. 92.

TIME AND BEAUTY

ONCE I was Laïs, in my beauty's prime
A very arrow in the hearts of all :
Behold me now, the Nemesis of Time.
Myself, O Queen of Love (but what art thou ?
Naught but an empty name on which I call !)
I know her not, the Laïs that is now.

IX. 260.

MAECIUS

Maecius, the author of thirteen epigrams, one being doubtful, probably belongs to the first century A.D., but nothing is known of his life.

BETRAYED

PHILAENIS, why lament and sigh?
   Sad tears your eyes bedew,
'Tis vain to tear your pretty hair,
   Tho' Strephon prove untrue.
The renegade, another maid
   Upon his bosom lies,
And false is he? yet trust in me,
   Who know love's remedies.
You weep, and though you whisper 'No,'
   Yet vainly you deny;
What words conceal your eyes reveal,
   And give your lips the lie.

v. 130.

MARCUS ARGENTARIUS

Marcus Argentarius belongs probably to some part of the first century A.D., but though two writers of the name are known to have existed, one being mentioned by Seneca and the other by Philostratus, it is not possible to identify the poet of the Anthology with either upon any certain evidence. There are thirty-seven epigrams extant under his name, all except one being included in the Palatine MS.

The epigram upon Hesiod has been a little expanded : the last couplet in the original means literally ' Casting the book on the ground I cried, " Why bring your works to me, old Hesiod ? " but the phrase underlined contains a play upon words which cannot be reproduced ; for it may mean ' give trouble ' as well as ' bring your works ': also the word ' Works ' is part of the title of Hesiod's book, which I have therefore given in full.

VELUT INTER IGNES LUNA MINORES

CROWN me ten cups for fair Lysidicè,
For dear Euphrantè more than one were vain—
Think ye from this she is less dear to me ?
Nay, by sweet Bacchus' life-blood that I drain !
Nay, she is tenfold dearer—in the skies
A myriad stars shall pale if Cynthia rise.

V. 110.

'WORKS AND DAYS'

ONE day I turned the page
Of Ascra's ancient sage
    To con his lore ;
But, seeing close at hand,
My dainty Pyrrha stand,
    His spell was o'er.
Casting the book aside,
' Old Hesiod,' I cried,
    ' Why plague me thus
With these, your musty lays,
Are not Love's "Works and Days
    Enough for us ?'

IX. 161.

PARMENIO

Parmenio was a Macedonian, and is credited with sixteen epigrams : he probably belongs to some part of the first century A.D., or a little later. The epigram upon the heroes of Thermopylae refers of course to the Persian exploits of bridging the Hellespont and cutting a canal round through the promontory of Athos.

'THE THREE HUNDRED'

THE changing paths of land and sea obeyed
    the Persian's nod ;
The earth bare up his navy, upon the wave he
    trod,
Till Spartan valour hurled him back on thrice
    an hundred spears.
O sea and rugged mountains, shame on your
    craven fears !

IX. 304.

G

STRATO

Strato of Sardis appears to have flourished during the reign of Hadrian (117-136 A.D.), and reference has been already made to the Anthology which he collected, from which the material of Section XII. is mainly taken. Some of the epigrams in this section, however, were added at a later date.

In addition to ninety-four poems in the section which bears his name, six other pieces by Strato are still extant; but many of his verses are offensive to taste, though they display great literary skill.

The longest of the epigrams here translated has been the subject of several versions and para-phrases, whilst other of his poems have been rendered, rather freely, by Merivale, Symonds, and Graves.

The second of the triolets is perhaps over free as a translation, though the sense is unaltered.

'GATHER YE ROSEBUDS'

IF your beauty must wane,
Now's the season to share it ;
For to hoard it were vain
If your beauty must wane.

If it last, then again
It were churlish to spare it ;
If your beauty must wane,
Now's the season to share it.

XII. 235.

RESTITUTION

IF my right you deny,
And I wronged you in this,
Let the statute apply ;
If my right you deny
Let 'an eye for an eye'
Mean 'a kiss for a kiss,'
If my right you deny,
And I wronged you in this.

XII. 188.

A KISS?

As we said 'Good-night' and the shadows fell,
You kissed me, or so I deem :
Was it really so—for I scarce can tell—
Or the cheat of a happy dream ?
Yet of all the rest not a line is blurred,
Or dim in my memory,

So well I recall your every word,
And all that you asked of me.
But if it were more than a dream divine,
The riddle to rede is this,
How tread I the earth, when the heaven
    is mine
For the worth of a single kiss ?

XII. 177.

LUCIAN

*Lucian of Samosata, best known for his Dia-
logues, flourished about 150 A.D. He lived to
an advanced age, and was still writing during the
reign of the Emperor Commodus (181-192 A.D.).*

ON A CHILD

WHEN I was five years old, and from grief I
    dwelt apart,
Hades snatched me away, he of the pitiless
    heart.
Wherefore weep not for me; as in life I had
    little share
So that little was good, for I knew not sorrow
    nor care.

VII. 308.

INSTABILITY

ALL things that mortals own must pass and die,
Or if they pass not yet we pass them by.

X. 31.

CLAUDIUS PTOLEMAEUS

*Claudius Ptolemaeus of Alexandria, the famous
Astronomer, flourished about the middle of the second
century of our era, and died, according to Suidas,
during the reign of Marcus. The epigram here
translated is the only one which can be attributed
to him with certainty, though there is another
headed Ptolemaeus amongst the sepulchral verses
which is in the form of an epitaph upon Timon
the Misanthrope, and runs thus :—*

> Stranger, you shall not hear my name,
>   Nor whence I came.
> I hope that you who pass me by
>   Right soon may die.

*The feeling that this poor epigram is unworthy
of the great astronomer is perhaps father to the
opinion that it is by another hand.*

THE THIRD HEAVEN

I KNOW myself a mortal man, the insect of a
    day ;
Yet gazing on the myriad stars that whirl upon
    their way,
Caught up to Zeus himself I spurn this petty
    earth aside,
And fed on food immortals use, my soul is
    satisfied.   IX. 577.

GLAUCUS

Glaucus of Nicopolis, the author of six epigrams, probably belongs to the third century A.D. The epitaph here translated is upon a sailor named Erasippus, and sounds like an echo of Propertius :

Sed tua nunc volucres adstant super ossa marinae,
Nunc tibi pro tumulo Carpathium omne mare.

a couplet imitated in the last two lines of Tennyson's 'Captain' ; the same idea is developed in the anonymous epitaph on Drake :

The waves became his winding sheet, the waters are
his tomb ;
But for his fame the ocean sea was not sufficient room.

'SI MONUMENTUM REQUIRIS'

UNDER the dust he is not pent,
No stone is above his grave,
But this wide sea is his monument,
For he sleeps beneath the wave.

He sank with his ship in a stormy sea
And his body moulders below ;
But none may tell where the place may be
For only the sea-gulls know.

VII. 285.

PALLADAS

*Palladas, of whose poems about 150 are pre-
served in the Anthology, probably belongs to the
end of the fourth and beginning of the fifth centuries A.D. Nothing is known certainly as
to his life, but he appears to have been a grammarian and a follower of the philosophy of
Hypatia (murdered in 415 A.D.), to whom one
of the epigrams attributed to him by Planudes is
devoted.*

*The voices of authority are by no means har-
monious as to Palladas' claims as a writer.
Casaubon calls him a tasteless versifier, and
Mr. J. A. Symonds speaks of his style as ' elegant
mediocrity by which he attained to the perfection
of Proverbial Philosophy in verse.'   On the other
hand, a critic in the Anthology says, ' Could the
screech-owl rival the nightingale, then might I
contend with Palladas ' ; whilst Mr. Mackail
compares his remorselessness to that of Swift.*

*Clearly, however, if the writer was a fourth
century Tupper, even his loftiest flights could
hardly raise him to the level of an Alexandrian
Swift, and imagination is too feeble to picture
the Dean of St. Patrick's tricked out in the paste
of elegant mediocrity.*

The first of the translations given here has been

attributed to St. Basil, but the fatalistic tone hardly suggests a Christian Father. The idea of No. 2 may be borrowed from Plato, but the comparison between life and a play is found again and again in the literature of many periods. The point of the satire upon Memphis the dancer lies, of course, in the stories of Daphne and Niobe, of whom the former was changed into a bay-tree and the latter into a stone. Ausonius develops the satire by adding two more lines :—

> 'Tis true in Canace his art was bad ;
> He didn't stab himself—we wish he had.

The first couplet of the lines on ' Fortune and Hope' occurs elsewhere in the Anthology as a separate epigram, and is thus translated by Robert Burton (1576-1640) :—

> Mine haven's found : fortune and hope adieu,
> Mock others now, for I have done with you.

But he seems to have taken this from Lyly's (1465-1573) version.

'DOWN THE STREAM'

THE stream that carries you doth carry all ;
    Bear and forbear, however fortune fall.
'Tis vain to strive and cry, whate'er you do ;
    The stream that carries all will carry you !

x. 73.

'MERELY PLAYERS'

LIFE's a game and a play,
So give heed to your part,
And put sadness away :
Life's a game and a play,
And in pain you shall pay
If you fail in your art ;
Life's a game and a play,
So give heed to your part.

X. 72.

A DEAD PEOPLE

ARE we not dead indeed, mere wraiths that
    seem,
  O sons of Greece, by evil fortune slain ?
For that we take for life is but a dream,
  The soul is fled, and how can life remain ?

X. 82.

PERFECTION

SAY not that snub-nosed Memphis dances ill,
For in two parts he shows a perfect skill ;
Is not his ' Daphne' stiff as any tree,
And starker than a stone his ' Niobe?'

XI. 255.

FORTUNE MY FOE

FORTUNE and Hope ! I bid you both ' good-
    bye.'
The way is found, no more for you I care ;
In human hearts the truth ye falsify,
Vain are the images ye picture there,
Dream phantoms of the things that never were,
False beacon lights that guide our course awry ;
Fortune and Hope, I bid you both ' good-bye.
The way is found, no more for you I care.
Cheat other men, vain Hope, for what reck I ?
Fools to delude are plenty and to spare ;
Fortune, thou dam of lies, thyself a lie,
No might is thine, thou art as empty air ;
Fortune and Hope, I bid you both ' good-bye.

IX. 134.

NAKED

NAKED I came on earth,
And naked shall I descend
Beneath her again ;
Naked is death as birth,
And as the beginning the end,
Why toil we in vain ?

X. 58.

THE LOST PAST

EACH day are we born again,
And never a jot doth remain
Of the life that is done.
We follow a diverse way
From the journey of yesterday
With each new sun.
To-day we begin to live,
Whatever the gods may give
Of life's residue.
Boast not the past your own,
Tho' many the years that are flown,
They are nothing to you.

x. 79.

THE LAST FEAR

THIS is the curse of life to fear to die,
And death's chief gain in losing fear doth lie:
Weep not for him that leaves the life of men,
'For death once dead there's no more dying
    then.'

x. 59.

'THOU HEAPEST UP RICHES'

THOU gatherest wealth—what profit shall it be?
Canst drag thy riches to the grave with thee?
Thou barterest time for gold—hast thou the
      power
To heap up life, or buy one added hour?

x. 60.

RESIGNATION

WHY toil, O man?   To strive with destiny
      Is little worth,
Since by the lot of fortune thou shalt be
      A slave from birth.
Yield thee to this, the fate the gods ordain,
      Flee strife and stress :
For, being man, the best that thou canst gain
      Is quietness.

x. 77.

GLYCON

*Glycon, whose only extant epigram is annexed
to those of Palladas, probably belongs to the same
period, but nothing whatever is known of his life.*

ILLUSION

ALL is dust, and a mocking dream,
  'All' and 'nothing' are just the same,
For nothing is, and the things that seem
  Out of a mindless chaos came.

x. 58.

AESOPUS

Aesopus, the author of only one epigram, which is translated below, is not the well-known fabulist of the name, but probably belongs to some part of the fourth century of our era. The epigram seems to be a paraphrase of a passage by Menander.

THE ILLS OF LIFE

How shall a man, O life, escape from thee,
Nor know death's pain? ten thousand ills are
    thine,
And hard it is to bear them or to flee :
For though the face of nature be divine,
The circling sun and moon, stars, earth, and
    sea,
Yet all beside is only pain and fear :
And if some good befall us, 'tis the sign
That answering Nemesis is lurking near.

X. 123.

MARIANUS

Marianus was a lawyer at Byzantium, and belongs to the end of the fifth and beginning of the sixth centuries. His chief claim to notoriety is that he turned the Idylls of Theocritus into Iambic verse; but there are six of his epigrams in the Anthology, one being supplied by Planudes, and the poem here translated was intended for inscription near a hot spring known as 'Eros's well.'

From this epigram—probably through an Italian or a French version—Shakespeare borrowed the idea of the two last sonnets—of which No. 154 is almost a translation, though the 'application' is supplied :—

SONNET CLIV

The little Love-god, lying once asleep,
Laid by his side his heart-inflaming brand,
Whilst many nymphs that vowed chaste life to
    keep
Came tripping by : but in her maiden hand
The fairest votary took up that fire
Which many legions of true hearts had warmed
And so the general of hot desire
Was sleeping by a virgin hand disarmed.
This brand she quenched in a cool well by,
Which from Love's fire took heat perpetual,
Growing a bath and healthful remedy

For men diseased : but I, my mistress' thrall,
Came there for cure, and this by that I prove,
Love's fire heats water, water cools not love.

LOVE'S WELL

'TWAS here, beneath the plane-tree's shade
That weary Love one day was laid,
And, overcome with gentle sleep,
He gave the nymphs his torch to keep.
So then they said to one another,
'Why dally we the flame to smother?
'Twere well if mortals' fierce desire
Could be extinguished with the fire.'
But when they tried the torch to cool,
It set afire the very pool ;
And they that strove the flame to quell,
Are serving-maids at Eros' well.

IX. 627.

THE HIGHEST LOVE

'WHERE is thy bended bow, and where thy store
Of shafts that leap to pierce the heart ?' I cried.
'Hast laid thy wings and grievous torch aside ?
I wist not that the son of Cypris bore

H

Three chaplets in his hand, or ever wore
So fair a crown as thine.   But he replied—
' I am not earth-born, passion deified,
That son of sensual joy whom men adore :
If hearts be clean, 'tis mine to kindle there
The white, pure flame of knowledge, and 'tis
    mine
To lead the souls of men to soar above :
Each chaplet is a virtue, and I bear
Three to bestow on man—and here doth shine
Wisdom, the Crown upon the brow of Love.'

XVI. 76.

PAUL

*Paul, the author of eighty epigrams in the
Anthology, was a Byzantine who held the court
office of Silentarius. He was contemporary with
Agathias, whose history mentions him, and since
two of the extant epigrams were written in reply
to others by the historian, we may conclude that
Paul belongs to the middle of the sixth century of
our era.*

*His best work is found in the section devoted
to love poems, and in these he is above all the
versifiers of his time; Mr. Symonds indeed
dismisses him in a sentence of half-regretful
contempt, but Jacobs claims for him genius beyond
his age, and he is worthy of at least as much
attention as some whose praise is in ' Studies of
the Greek Poets.' Much of the verse of this period
is vile in more respects than one : but the epigrams
here translated (and their number might easily
be increased) seem to me to be free from the taint
which sickened Mr. Symonds.*

*The huitain on p. 116 has been translated many
times, and the imaginary epitaph, p. 119, is well
known in the version of Cowper which runs thus :—*

> My name, my country, what are they to thee?
> What, whether base or proud my pedigree?
> Perhaps I far surpassed all other men,
> Perhaps I fell below them all: what then?

Suffice it, stranger, that thou see'st a tomb,
Thou know'st its use, it hides — no matter
whom!

I have ventured to translate it again in the hope
of getting nearer to the Greek and emphasising
the fact that it is as it were a dialogue between the
tombstone and the reader.

THE BOND-MAN

SHE plucked a thread of golden hair
    To bind my hands in merry glee,
And first I mocked the fetter fair,
    Frail sign of brief captivity.
    But ah! no might could set me free;
As triple brass the bond doth hold,
    I follow where she guideth me,
Led by a single hair of gold.

V. 234.

ON THE WINGS OF THE MORNING

(SENT WITH A PEARL)

WHAT though your wandering feet
    To a distant land should fare?
Borne on the pinions fleet
    Of love I will find you there;

Flee to the dawn, if you will,
  That hath love's own blush on her face,
Yet will I follow you still
  O'er measureless miles of space.
Spurn not the gift that I bring
  From the depths of the ocean caves,
This is the offering
  Of her that was born of the waves ;
This she sends you in token
  Of grace more fair than her own,
For Paphia's pride is broken,
  To you she doth yield her throne.

V. 301.

DISARMED

LET no man dread the archer more,
  Nor fear to feel his dart ;
Impetuous Love hath spent his store,
  And all upon my heart.

Henceforward none should be dismayed,
  No wingèd god is he,
For love long since his flight hath stayed
  To set his foot on me.

Here rests he still, he cannot stir,
　　For time no respite brings,
And so full well may I aver
　　That Love hath cast his wings.

v. 268.

UNADORNED

A ROSE to me doth need no garland's grace,
　　Nor you, my queen, rich robes or jewels rare
　　Your throat is whiter than the pearls you wear
Set on your locks the richest gold is base ;
Seeing your eyes, the bluebell hides her face ;
　　Your mouth's a dewy bud, but not so fair
　　　　　　A rose to me.

That breast the zone of Cypris should embrace
　　But all these glories drive me to despair,
　　Save only your dear, gentle eyes—for there
The first faint ray of hope, which now I trace,
　　　　　　Arose to me.

v. 270.

LOVEBOUND

OFT as I strove to say ' good-bye '
　　The word half uttered died ;
Love curbed my tongue, and here am I
　　Still constant at your side.

To dwell apart from that dear light
  That on my soul hath shone,
Methinks were as the bitter night
  That broods o'er Acheron.

Yours is the light whereby I live,
  Dearer than day to me,
For that is voiceless, and you give
  Sunshine and melody.

Sweeter than Siren songs of old
  Is that belovèd voice,
And all my hopes, by this controlled,
  Must languish or rejoice.

V. 241.

THE EPITAPH—AND THE READER

My name and country were . . . . no matter
  what !
Noble my race . . . . who cares though it were
  not ?
The fame I won in life . . . . is all forgot !
Now here I lie . . . . and no one cares a jot !

VII. 307.

RONDEAU

O FOOLISH eyes, why rashly dare
To drain Love's nectar?   Too divine,
Too potent far is Beauty's wine,
And hazardous for you to share ;
Flee hence, and in a calmer air
Peace offerings pour at Cypris' shrine,
          O foolish eyes !
If still the frenzy plague me, bear
For ever both your pangs and mine,
Bedewed with tears, love's bitter brine
You lit the flame, you laid the snare,
          O foolish eyes.

v. 226.

AT SUNRISE

WHEN yesternight in Love's despite
  My lady shut me out,
With bitter tongue a gibe she flung
  My misery to flout.

An idle word was that I heard,
  'From scorn the loves will flee';
But lo her pride the saw belied
  And fanned the flame in me !

I swore to stay a year away,
    And stoop no more to sue ;
But with the morn am I forsworn,
    And come again to woo.

                                    v. 256.

RUFINUS

Rufinus belongs to the same period as Paul the Silentiary, and like him held office in the Imperial Court where he was ' Domestic.'

About forty of his epigrams are extant in the Anthology, all of which are in the section devoted to love poems, and many show a pretty taste and skill.

The epigram on p. 123 has been translated by the author of Ionica, but not, I think, in his best manner. The version begins thus :—

> Flowers my fingers have been weaving,
> Rhodoclea, you're receiving.

The original is rather like Waller's famous lines, but of course the comparison of beauty to a flower is common to all ages and lands. The original of the love letter on p. 124 uses the Greek forms of address and subscription, commonly used in letters, very cleverly, but to reproduce these is not easy. The difference in meaning between this and other versions is due to the adoption of various readings—for example, Mr. Mackail adapts Hecker's emendation, and I have followed the interpretation of Grotius.

The epigram on Love and Wine, p. 124, has been translated by Moore with a sort of chirpy vivacity

*which hardly represents the mock heroic tone of
the original* :—

> With reason I cover my breast as a shield,
> And fearlessly meet little Love in the field.
> Thus meeting his godship I 'll ne'er be dis-
>   mayed,
> But if Bacchus should ever advance to his aid,
> Alas, then unable to combat the two,
> Unfortunate warrior, what shall I do?

> ' *Comme a ceste fleur la viellesse
> Fera ternir vostre beauté.*'

LAI

> THESE blossoms fair
> I wreathed, my love, for thee ;
> Violet and lily see,
> Narcissus rare,
> Rose and anemone,
> A gift for Rhodoclé
> To deck her hair ;
> And, though they withered be,
> Yet treat them tenderly ;
> From scorn forbear,
> Since by the gods' decree,
> All fair mortality
> That fate must share.

v. 74.

A LOVE LETTER TO ELPIS

GOOD MORROW, dear, if any 'good' can be
When you are far from me ;
This dreary severance I cannot bear—
Nay, by your eyes I swear
Of mighty Artemis to seek relief ;
These tears will show my grief,
To-morrow I would fly to home, and you ;
Ten thousand times adieu.

V. 9.

LOVE AND WINE

AGAINST Love's dart I arm my heart,
    And reason is my shield.
I do not fear to meet with him
    Alone upon the field.
Though mortal yet, I dare to set
    Man's might against a god's,
But what if Bacchus join with love ?
    I dare not face the odds.

V. 93.

'LOVE IN HER SUNNY EYES DOES DANCING PLAY'

PURE is her cheek as crystal, in her eyes
   The sunlight glows,
And on her lips a fairer colour lies
   Than decks the rose ;
Her throat and breast have marble's purity ;
   Nay, I aver,
Not silver-footed Thetis of the sea
   Could vie with her.
Mark you amid the glory of her hair
   One gleam of white ?
I deem it but a spray of white-thorn there,
   A new delight.

v. 48.

'GODDESSES THREE'

OF late again for pride of place
   Three lovely dames contended,
And each would claim her form and face
   As most to be commended.

As there they stood, the Heavenly Three
  Could scarcely match their beauty,
And, needing one their judge to be,
  They laid on me the duty.

But knowing Paris' fate of old,
  So soon as I had seen them,
From none the crown would I withhold,
  But gave the prize between them.

v. 36.

A BARGAIN

O EROS, if your aim be fair,
Right gladly as a god I'll own you,
For you must pierce us both, or spare,
O Eros, if your aim be fair.
But favour either, then I swear
You're but a cheat, and I'll dethrone you
O Eros, if your aim be fair,
Right gladly as a god I'll own you.

v. 97.

SANS MERCI

FAIR Prodicé I chanced to meet,
  When none was by to see,
And fell before her pretty feet
  Her suppliant to be.

'Save me,' I cried, ' sweet maid, or soon
　　This fluttering life must wane,
But only you can grant the boon,
　　And bid me live again.'

She wept to hear my tale of woe,
　　But soon her tears she dried,
Then raised her hand,—to aid me? No !
　　To thrust me more aside.

v. 66.

AGATHIAS

Agathias, son of Mamnonius, who was born at Myrina in Asia Minor, flourished during the reign of Justinian, being thus contemporary with Paul the Silentiary, Rufinus, and Macedonius. Mention has been made of the Anthology which he published, but in addition to this he compiled a history of events during the years 553-559 A.D., which breaks off abruptly at the latter date. The book was written after the death of Justin II. in 578 A.D., and from this it would appear that Agathias was younger than his friend Paul.

During his early life he studied law, which he found distasteful, so returning to his native place he devoted himself to its improvement, becoming, as he boasts, ' father to the town, and making her the envy of all who was aforetime their scorn.'

Besides the epigrams, ninety-seven in number, Agathias published a volume of poems entitled Daphniaca, of which the dedication to Aphrodite (Pal. Anth., VI. 80) is translated below.

THE DEDICATION OF HIS BOOK

NINE books of song, O Paphian Queen,
Agathias dedicates to thee :
Since Eros' rites my theme have been,
The lofty Muses love not me.

And now thy bard doth make his plea
   That, in return for all his care,
Thou bid him live heart-whole and free,
   Or love a maiden kind as fair.

VI. 80.

AGE, THE AVENGER

So proud is lovely Rhodope
   That, if I say ' Good morn,'
She scarce will deign to answer me,
   But lifts her brow for scorn.

Her portals with a wreath I crown,
   And lo ! in angry pride,
She casts the pretty garland down
   And spurns the flowers aside.

Come, wrinkled age, be pitiless,
   The haughty fair subdue :
The pride that heeds not my distress
   May yield at least to you !

V. 92.

LAÏS

UPON the road to Corinth I espied
A grave by the wayside
Bearing the name of Laïs, and I shed
A tear for beauty dead :

I

' All hail, sweetheart,' I said, ' for Laïs' name
Lives on the lips of fame,
And I that never saw you in your bloom,
Have pity on your doom.
So many hearts of old were stricken through,
Fairest, for love of you—
But now you dwell a ghost by Lethe's mere,
Your beauty mouldering here.'

VII. 220.

' TROJA RENASCENS '

STRANGER, deride me not,
Though Spartan-born, child of mine ancient foe ;
Fallen am I, but many share my woe,
        By Fortune's even lot ;

    Nor mourn my fate forlorn
Though we be kin, if Asia gave thee birth,
My sons have empire over all the earth,
        For Rome is Trojan born.

    Though I be desolate,
And in the dust the towers that once were mine
My palaces, and every holy shrine,
        Cast down by envious hate,

Once more a queen am I,
And thou, my daughter, Rome that know'st not
    fear,
Stretch forth thine hand and 'neath thy rod
    austere
        Justly let Hellas lie.

                    IX. 155.

THE HEALER

WHY fear ye Death who is the sire of peace,
Healing the ills of poverty and pain?
He comes but once, and who hath won release
Shall never fear to see his face again;
But many ills must living mortals bear,
Each in his turn, and divers forms they wear.

                    X. 69.

'A KISS WITHIN THE CUP'

I LOVE not wine, but if you choose
    That I drink deep to you,
The cup I'll drain if you but deign
    To set your lips thereto.
When beauty's kiss hath crowned the draught
    No sullen churl am I;
Your hand divine has poured the wine?
    I'll drain the goblet dry.

So shall the cup transfer to me
    The grace it late did win,
And bid me share the nectar rare
    Your kiss hath left therein.

v. 261.

THE MEAN

IN love? then play a gallant part;
    Though prostrate it be lying,
Yet think not you can nerve your heart
    With constant prayer and sighing.

But sometimes wear a sterner mien,
    A frown the fair may soften;
Nor let your longing gaze be seen
    To rest on her too often.

Yet 'tis a woman's way to scorn
    All over-haughty graces,
To mock a lover too forlorn,
    And laugh in rueful faces;

And best the swain shall win success
    Who doth the mean discover;
For mingled pride and tenderness
    Shall make a lucky lover.

v. 216.

LEONTIUS

Leontius, to whom twenty-six epigrams are ascribed—two being doubtfully authentic—is supposed to be the Leontius Referendarius (the title of a legal official) who is known to have lived in the time of Justinian. Twelve of his epigrams occur in Planudes only, perhaps owing to the loss of the section in the Palatine MS. which contained verses upon works of art.

The 'Plato' here mentioned is not the philosopher, but a harpist of the name, of whom nothing further is known.

TO A DEAD MUSICIAN

WHEN Orpheus died song was not wholly dead,
   She lived in you,
Plato ; but in the hour your spirit fled,
   Music died too.
A fragment of the melodies of old
   Dwelt in your soul,
A treasure that no other shrine could hold
   Nor hand control.

       VII. 571.

DAMASCIUS

Damascius belongs to the reign of Justinian. The couplet here translated is the only one of his epigrams which survives. He was a Neoplatonist and suffered exile under the penal laws against Pagans, but was afterwards specially exempted from their operation.

FREED!

O ZOSIMA, your soul was ever free,
And now your body too hath liberty.

VII. 553.

MACEDONIUS

*Macedonius of Thessalonica, generally called
' the Consul,' flourished during the reign of
Justinian, being thus contemporary with Paul,
Rufinus, and Agathias, but nothing is known as
to the details of his life. Forty-three epigrams
are attributed to him in the Palatine MS., and
one more occurs in Planudes only.*

*Fourteen of the epigrams are in the erotic
section, and these are perhaps the best to read:
of the rest the majority are either dedications or
verses upon gay or convivial themes. The only
sepulchral inscription by him is here translated,
p. 137.*

HOPE DEFERRED

' TO-MORROW come '—must I always hear
    The sound of that dreary word ?
To-morrow is never *to-day*, my dear,
And your only boon to my love sincere
    Is the gift of hope deferred.

You are kind to others, but not to me,
    And my heart is left to grieve :
Yet age and wrinkles are ill to see,
So think what the evening of life may be,
    When you say To-morrow at eve.

v. 233.

THE VINTAGE

THEY gather the vintage year by year,
Nor scorn the grape for a tendril sere,
O heart's dear treasure, your arms and mine
Are the strong, soft bond that our love doth
    twine ;
And I gather the grapes of love, nor care—
Since yours is the dower of all things fair—
For another summer or spring's young grace ;
But if wrinkled Time should strive to trace
His tendril mark on your loveliness,
I should not heed it, or love you less.

v. 227.

TO THE MORNING STAR

O PHOSPHOR, hurt not Love, nor learn
    Of Mars his cruel art,
Though next to thine his star may burn,
    Lest thou be hard of heart.

Thou sawest Phaëthon within
  The bower of Clymenè,
But didst not haste thy goal to win,
  So now be kind to me.

So long I sighed ! ah, stay thy flight,
  And let thy course be slow ;
May this be longer than the night
  The far Cimmerians know.

v. 223.

WHITHER—AND WHENCE?

I BID thee farewell, O Earth,
  Who shalt cover me ;
Farewell, O goddess of Birth,
  I began from thee.
This part of the way is done,
  And I needs must go,
But a course is yet to run
  That I cannot know.
Nay, who shall that course control ?
  For never I knew
What or whence was the soul
  That hath dwelt with you.

vii. 556.

THEODORUS

Theodorus, date unknown; only three of his epigrams are extant.

ON A DEAD JESTER

STERN Pluto, when you reached him, smiled
    and said—
' O Tityrus, be jester to the dead !'

VII. 566.

DIOPHANES

*Diophanes of Myrina (date unknown) is repre-
sented by one couplet only, and this is imperfect,
the second line being added to the Palatine MS.
in another hand. The epigram is in hendeca
syllabics.*

AN INDICTMENT

Love's a thief from of old,
    If you judge him aright ;
For three reasons I hold
Love's a thief from of old :
He is sleepless, and bold,
    And he steals his delight.
Love's a thief from of old,
    If you judge him aright.

                                    v. 309.

CAPITO

Capito, date unknown. This is the only surviving epigram.

BEAUTY AND CHARM

ALTHOUGH upon a lovely face the eye delight
    to look,
Yet what is beauty lacking grace? a bait without
    a hook.

v. 67.

THE ANONYMOUS EPIGRAMS

MASTERLESS

The couplet from which this is translated occurs twice in the Anthology : first by itself in XI. 53, *and secondly in a quatrain of Alcaeus. It seems probable that its proper place is in the latter.*

THE ROSE AND THE THORN

A LITTLE while do roses reign,
For perfect beauty may not last ;
Then, seeking, you shall seek in vain.
A little while do roses reign—
But ah ! the cruel thorns remain,
Though the fair flowers be overpast.
A little while do roses reign,
For perfect beauty may not last.

XI. 53.

'NOT OF ITSELF'

This is often quoted as the original of verse two of Ben Jonson's ' Drink to me only with thine eyes,' which, however, is really taken from Philostratus.

ALTHOUGH I send a perfume rare,
'Tis not of grace to you I send it,
The gain is to the gift I swear,
Although I send a perfume rare :
'Twill earn a sweeter fragrance there
Than any power but yours could lend it ;
Although I send a perfume rare,
'Tis not of grace to you I send it.

v. 91.

EPITAPH ON CLEOETES

This epitaph is not in the Anthology, but the original inscription is still preserved in the Museum at Athens : it belongs to sixth century B.C.

DEAD is Cleoetes, Menesaechmus' son ;
    Can pity be denied,
When thou dost look upon the tomb of one
    Who was so fair, and died ?

ON A BABY

This epitaph is upon a tombstone preserved in Rome, and above it is written 'D.M.S. Ti. Claudia Eugenetis vixit annos Xi. dies X.   Ti Claudius Anicetus pater fecit.'   A Greek inscription follows upon Menecrates, son of Apollonius. who died at four years and four months old, and it is to him that the epitaph translated here refers.

I HAD set but my lips to life when Hades
  snatched me away,
But whether for good or ill it is not mine to say.
Shame on thy greed, O Death ! Why needest
  thou come so fast
To ravish mine infant life ? we are all thine own
  at the last.

App. II. 337.

WITH A PRESENT OF A PEN

These lines were sent to Leontion with a present of a silver pen.   The wording of the original is slightly expanded in accordance with what I believe to be the meaning. The literal sense of the second couplet is ' So well, fair Leontion, hath Athene dowered thee with excellent skill, and so well Cypris with the excellence of beauty.'

I WAS but silver when I came
New moulded from the maker's flame,
But what your hand shall deign to hold
Shall surely turn to purest gold.
Since Pallas gave you wisdom's dower,
And Cypris beauty's fairest flower,
No marvel there should seem to be,
Nor magic in this alchemy.

XVI. 324.

TRIOLETS

*This and the next epigram, so similar in idea,
are put together by some editors, and others add
to these a couplet of Theophanes, whose meaning is
'Would that I were a white lily that thou mightest
hold me close and satisfy me.' There is no authority for this arrangement, which was due to Grotius.
There is a modern Greek version of this epigram
which will be found in Paton's ' Anth. Graecae
Erotica,' and Dr. Hawtrey's French translations
run thus :*

RONDEAUX

I

Heureux zephyr,
Que je t'envie
Ce douce plaisir
Quand ma Célie

Découvre au soleil la blancheur
D'un cou d'ivoire, avec ton aile
D'en modérer l'ardeur,
 Et là, fidèle,
 Pouvoir mourir,
 Heureux Zephyr !

II

 Rose plus fortunée
 De cette main touchée,
Toi qui pourra t'épanouir
Sur ce beau sein que la cruelle
A mes yeux jamais ne rêvêle,
 Et là mourir
 De cette main touchée,
 Rose plus fortunée.
     DR. E. C. HAWTREY.

I

If I were but a gentle air,
And you were wandering by the sea.
So haply I should meet you there,
If I were but a gentle air,
And lightly kiss that bosom fair—
For you would turn your heart to me,
If I were but a gentle air,
And you were wandering by the sea.
     v. 83.

K

II

IF I were but a blushing rose,
And your dear hand should gather me,
Then should I win a fair repose,
If I were but a blushing rose.
That breast whose whiteness mocks the snows
The haven where I fain would be,
If I were but a blushing rose,
And your dear hand should gather me !

v. 84.

A POSY

*The original couplet is inscribed upon an onyx,
and is not in the Anthology. There is some doubt
as to the reading of the second line.*

LOVE me, that love you so,
    And I shall owe
To love a double due :
Hate me, and all your hate
    Were not so great
As is my love for you.

App. III. 149.

ON A NAMELESS GRAVE

In the MS., part of an epigram by Simonides
is annexed to the couplet which is here translated
—this is, however, only a clerical blunder.

O SAILOR, ask not whose the tomb may be,
But Fortune grant to you a kindlier sea.

VII. 350.

A PRAYER

The original is found in the second Alcibiades
of Plato as well as in the Anthology. ' I think,'
says Socrates, ' that the poet was wise, who having,
as I suppose, foolish friends whom he saw pray-
ing for things which it were not better for them
to have, made this general prayer on behalf of
them all.'   Mr. J. A. Symonds seems to interpret
the prayer as having a more restricted sense, for
he translates it :—

> God grant us good, whether or not we pray,
> But e'en from praying souls keep bad away.'

O ZEUS, our King, all good to us fulfil,
    Whether or no we pray ;
And when unwittingly we ask for ill,
    Keep thou that ill away.

X. 108.

A PYTHIAN ORACLE

The original of this is entitled ' An Oracle given by the Pythian priestess,' and there are several to the same effect.

PURE is this temple, wouldst thou enter in?
  Pure be thy soul from sin.
Fair water from the nymphs' clear brook should
  be
  Cleansing enough for thee :
If thou be good thou needest nothing more,
  Some little sprinkling pour—
But all the ocean's flood may not efface
  Guilt from the heart that's base.

        XIV. 71.

REMEMBER

The title of the original is ' To Sabinus, in Corinth,' but no author's name is given, though Grotius, upon no known authority, ascribes it to S. Gregory. Ovid has developed the idea of the last couplet :—

  Non ego, securae biberes si pocula Lethes,
  Excidere haec credam pectore posse tuo.

THIS monument, Sabinus,
  Your friend has raised to you,

A thing too frail to tell the tale
   Of all the love we knew.
My heart seeks yours, and in the grave,
   If memory yet may be,
Drink not the draught of Lethe's flood,
   But still remember me.

                        VII. 346.

AN INSCRIPTION AT BESANÇON

*This epitaph is not in the Anthology, but is
extant upon a tombstone found at Rome and now
in the Museum at Besançon. The inscription is
much defaced, but was copied whilst still legible.*

THIS tomb was builded by thy loving hand,
   Oceanus the wise, dear husband mine,
Wherefore my dust is glad ; in shadow-land
   'Tis music to my soul, that love of thine.
Through life remember me ; pour on my shrine
   Lost Love's libation, and for sorrow weep ;
Yet weeping say, ' Popilia is asleep.'
   The good die not, theirs is a sleep divine.

                       App. II. 289.

A LIFE HISTORY

The couplet of which this is a translation is inscribed upon the neck of a bust, now in the Museum at Bologna, which also bears two other inscriptions: (1) 'Be joyful if thou be just'; (2) 'My son, be cautious lest thou babble: verily the tongue only toileth in vain when it doth speak, but if it run astray it bringeth many an evil.'

The figure is said to be a Hermes, but judging from the description this does not seem likely, and the suggestion has been made that it may represent Democritus.

TIME was I was not: I began to be,
I was, and am not; that's the end of me;
He lies that doth a fuller knowledge feign,
For I, that am not, shall not be again.

App. II. 427.

A WORN TARGET

There is a good deal of confusion as to the authorship of this epigram. In the Palatine MS. it is headed 'Unknown or Archias.' In Planudes it is united to a couplet by Capito, and the epigram thus compounded is ascribed to Nicarchus.

LOVE must find a fresh heart
    As a mark for his bow,
If he 'd practise his art.
Love must find a fresh heart,
    For in mine every part
Has its arrow to show ;
Love must find a fresh heart
    As a mark for his bow.

                                    v. 98.

ON A NIOBE OF PRAXITELES

*This epigram was borrowed by Ausonius, whose
version* (Ep. XXVIII.) *runs thus :—*

Vivebam ; sum facta silex, quae deinde polita
    Praxitelis manibus, vivo iterum Niobe,
Reddidit artificis manus omnia, sed sine sensu ;
    Hunc ego, quum laesi numina, non habui.

FROZEN to stone, my living flesh obeyed,
    Of old, the gods' decree :
Now of that stone Praxiteles hath made
    A living Niobe.

                                XVI. 129.

ON A LITTLE CHILD

O HADES, death's inexorable king,
Wilt never turn aside from plundering?
   Now is Callaeschrus of his life bereft.
And what avails to know the child shall be
A plaything in thy halls, Persephone,
   When sorrow broods above the home he left?

VII. 483.

'STREW ON HER ROSES'

LET blossoms deck the mound that covers you,
   Nor barren briar nor evil weed be there,
But violets and narcissus wet with dew,
   Sweet marjoram and roses everywhere.

Anon. Kaibel. E., IX. 548.

THE SWALLOW SONG OF RHODES

*' The swallow song of Rhodes' is quoted by
Athenaeus, who, relying on the authority of
Theognis, says that in the month of Boedromion
children went round begging and singing this
song. It is, of course, traditional, and not assign-
able to any author.*

THE swallow is here, 'tis the prime of the year,
   She brings the hours of delight;

See the glossy black of the robe on her back,
  And the gleam on her breast of white.

Then give us a cake for the swallow's sake,
  You have ample store of these ;
She is willing to dine upon bread and wine,
  Or even a dish of cheese.

She will not despise an humble prize,
  But even an egg will do ;
Then don't say ' No ' if you 'd have us go,
  Or still we will pester you.

We will plunder the store, and force the door,
  Or carry it clean away,
Lintel and post, of the churlish host
  Who grudges a gift to-day.

From the ingleside we will steal his bride
  As she sits demurely there ;
To take her too is little to do,
  For she 's dainty and light as air.

Bring out your best to the little guest,
  No cause have you to fear,
For children follow the wake of the swallow,
  There 's never a grey-beard here.

                        ATHENAEUS, VIII. 60.

9 781589 638143